KU-017-695

DK EYEWITNESS TOP 10 TRAVEL GUIDES

AMSTERDAM

MAIN CONTRIBUTORS
FIONA DUNCAN & LEONIE GLASS

DORLING KINDERSLEY
LONDON • NEW YORK • MUNICH
MELBOURNE • DELHI
WWW.DK.COM

Left **Hollandse Manege** Right **Magere Brug**

A DORLING KINDERSLEY BOOK

www.dk.com

Produced by DP Services,
31 Ceylon Road, London W14 0PY

Reproduced by Colourscan, Singapore
Printed and bound in Italy by Graphicom

First published in Great Britain in 2003
by Dorling Kindersley Limited
80 Strand, London WC2R 0RL
A Penguin Company

**Copyright 2003 © Dorling
Kindersley Limited, London**

A CIP catalogue record is available from
the British Library.

ISBN 0 7513 4845 7

Within each Top 10 list in this book, no
hierarchy of quality or popularity is
implied. All 10 are, in the editor's
opinion, of roughly equal merit.

Contents

Amsterdam's Top 10

Left **Eerste Klas Café, Centraal Station** Right **Prinsengracht**

Contents

Left **Café de Jaren** Right **Montelbaanstoren, Oude Schans**

AMSTERDAM'S
TOP 10

AMSTERDAM'S TOP 10

ᵀᴼᴾ10 Amsterdam Highlights

Amsterdam has an appeal that is absolutely unique. It's a vibrant place, a treasure-trove of extraordinary artistic riches, and the living embodiment of 900 years of history, during which it rose to become the centre of a huge global empire. After a period of decline, it matured into today's relaxed and tolerant modern metropolis. Elegant and serene, Amsterdam also has its seamy side, and this too is part of its character, as much as its famous network of canals. Whatever you are looking for, this small city packs a big punch.

Canals and Waterways **1**

Amsterdam's canals – in particular, the elegant ring of three 17th-century canals known as the Grachtengordel – are its defining feature *(see pp8–11)*.

2 Rijksmuseum

The country's largest national museum houses an unrivalled collection of 17th-century Dutch art, and much besides. Vermeer's *Milkmaid (left)* and Rembrandt's *Night Watch* are among the star sights *(see p12–15)*.

Van Gogh Museum **3**

The Van Gogh Museum houses simply the most comprehensive collection of the artist's work to be seen anywhere in the world – including some of his most famous paintings. The collection also includes works by other 19th-century artists *(see pp16–19)*.

4 Museum Amstelkring

Things are not always what they seem, and that is certainly true of this gem of a 17th-century house set in the unlikely surroundings of the Red Light District: tucked away on its upper floors is a rare example of a perfectly preserved clandestine Catholic church. The rest of the museum is fascinating, too – the interior has changed little since the Golden Age *(see pp20–21)*.

Map labels: Brouw, Jordaan, Prinsengracht, Keizersgracht, Bloemgracht, ROZENGRACHT, RAADHUISSTRAA, KEIZERSGRACHT, Jordaan, Negen Straatjes, MARNIXSTRAAT, NASSAUKADE, LEIDSESTRAAT, Keizer, LEIDSE PLEIN, Prinsengr, Lijnbaansgrac, WETERINGSCHANS, STADHOUDERSKADE, HOBBEMAST, VAN BAERLESTRAAT, PAULUS POTTER STR, MUSEUM PLEIN, HOBBEMAKADE, STADHO, 9, 2, 3

5 Begijnhof
A haven of peace, the Begijnhof was built as a refuge for the Beguines, a lay Catholic sisterhood. Amsterdam's oldest house is here *(see pp22–3)*.

6 Amsterdams Historisch Museum
Housed in the old city orphanage, this vibrant collection traces the history of Amsterdam from the 12th century *(see pp24–7)*.

7 Oude Kerk
This great Gothic basilica preserves a number of its treasures, despite being stripped of its paintings and statuary during the Iconoclasm *(see pp28–9)*.

we
le

Oosterdok

NIEUW MARKT

Oude Zijde

Oudeschans

Wertheim Park

Artis Plantage

AMSTEL REMBRANDT PLEIN

FREDERIKS PLEIN

500 ⌐ yards ⌐ 0 ⌐ metres ⌐ 500

8 Museum Van Loon
Visitors to the Van Loon family residence on the Keizersgracht, lovingly restored in the style of the mid-18th century, have a rare opportunity to see behind the façade of a grand canal house – and to wander freely about it *(see pp30–31)*.

9 Anne Frankhuis
The hiding place of Anne Frank and her family, before they were discovered, arrested and sent to their deaths, is today a deeply moving museum *(see pp32–3)*.

10 Dam Square
This is where it all started: Amsterdam's main square is on the site of the dam on the Amstel around which the city grew. Now it hosts markets, events and all shades of city life *(see pp34–5)*.

🔟 Canals and Waterways

With their delightful views, pretty bridges (1,281 in all), idiosyncratic gabled houses and relaxed waterside cafés, Amsterdam's 75 km (47 miles) of canals are great fun to explore: full of interest and perfect for a leisurely stroll. They are a constant reminder that the Netherlands is the world's flattest country, half of which has been reclaimed from the sea with the aid of dykes, canals and, more recently, huge tidal barriers. Before you start exploring Amsterdam's canals on foot, however, you should take a boat tour (see pp10 and 136) for a fascinating overview.

Café Van Puffelen

🍺 Three perfect canalside cafés are Papeneiland, at Prinsengracht 2, Van Puffelen, where you can sit on a barge in summer *(see p102)*, and De Sluyswacht *(see p80)*.

✪ If you are in the centre of Amsterdam, with no time to explore the city's canals, at least take a stroll to the Huis op de Drie Grachten, (House on Three Canals), step-gabled on all three of its canal-facing sides, at Oudezijds Voorburgwal 249.

Top 10 Canals and Waterways

1. Herengracht
2. Keizersgracht
3. Prinsengracht
4. Entrepotdok
5. Reguliersgracht
6. Amstel River
7. Brouwersgracht
8. Bloemgracht
9. Leidsegracht
10. Singel

1 Herengracht
Stateliest canal of the Grachtengordel *(see p11)*, the Herengracht is famous for its Golden Bend – a grand but rather lifeless stretch of mansions built for the richest merchants. A more beautiful stretch lies between Huidenstraat and Leidsestraat, best viewed from the east side.

2 Keizersgracht
The central canal of the Grachtengordel has fine stretches between Brouwersgracht and Raadhuisstraat, and again between Runstraat and Leidestraat.

3 Prinsengracht
The outermost canal of the Grachtengordel, designed for warehouses and artisans' housing, has a breezy, laid-back air. It is peppered with cafés, art galleries and houseboats. Cycle its 3 km (2 mile) length, or explore short stretches on foot.

Entrepotdok
4 An imposing stretch of former dockland has been restored to provide offices and apartments, with outdoor cafés overlooking colourful houseboats.

Reguliersgracht
5 Much loved for its pretty houses and hump-backed bridges, Reguliersgracht was cut in 1664. Look out for Nos 57, 59 and 63.

Amstel River
6 Until the construction of the Grachtengordel pushed it out of focus, the river Amstel was the city's *raison d'être*. It is still used by barges to transport goods to the city's port.

Brouwersgracht
7 The happy-go-lucky feel of the "brewers' canal' makes a pleasant contrast to the sophisticated elegance of the Grachtengordel.

Bloemgracht
8 A charming canal crossed by cast-iron bridges, Bloemgracht is known locally as "the Herengracht of the Jordaan", because of its elaborately gabled houses.

Leidsegracht
9 This lovely – and exclusive – canal was cut in 1664, when it was the main barge route from Amsterdam to Leiden.

Singel
10 Once a fortified moat, the Singel is now home to Bloemenmarkt, the domed Ronde Lutherse Kerk and the soaring Neo-Gothic Krijtberg church.

How Amsterdam's Houses are Built

Each house is built on wooden piles sunk into the marshy, porous subsoil. It wasn't until the 17th century, when the piles could be sunk deep enough to reach the hard layer of sand that lies at 13 m (42 ft), that any real stability was achieved. Some reach even further, to a second layer of sand at 18 m (58 ft). If piles come into contact with air, they rot, so today, concrete is used instead of wood.

Left **Canal tour boat on the Oude Schans** Right **De Poezenboot**

Unexpected Sights on a Canal Tour

1 The Safest Vaults
The vaults of the Dutch National Bank are sunk some 15 m (48 ft) below ground level. In the event of an alarm, they have been designed to allow the waters of the Singelgracht to flood into them.

2 The Prison Bridge
The Torensluis – the widest bridge in Amsterdam – spans the Singel on the site of a 17th-century sluice gate. A lock-up jail was built into its foundations.

3 The Cat Boat
Hundreds of feline waifs and strays are given refuge in *De Poezenboot* (The Cat Boat), moored on the Singel *(above)*.

4 The Drunken Tsar
In 1716, Peter the Great got drunk at his friend Christoffel Brants' house at Keizersgracht 317, and kept the mayor waiting at a civic reception. That night, he stayed at the house of the Russian ambassador, Herengracht 527, where Napoleon also stayed in 1811.

Peter the Great

5 The Narrowest House
Is Singel 7 the smallest house in Amsterdam? No, it's simply the back door of a wedge-shaped house, whatever your tour guide tells you.

6 The Oldest Café
Which is really the oldest café in Amsterdam? It's Café Chris, in Bloemstraat, dating from 1624. A curiosity: the loo is flushed from the bar.

7 The Most Crooked Café
Teetering Café de Sluyswacht, built in 1695, makes an alarming sight as you glide by along the Oude Schans *(see p80)*.

8 The Wrapped-up House
Look carefully at Victoria Hotel, near the station, and you will see two tiny 17th-century houses embedded in the monumental 19th-century façade. A little old lady, so the story goes, refused to sell up, so the hotel had to wrap itself around them.

9 The Floating Pagoda
The vast Sea Palace, Amsterdam's famous floating Chinese restaurant, makes an unusual sight in Oosterdok. With its twinkling lights and many windows, it makes a romantic dinner spot.

10 The Tower of Tears
This medieval defensive tower has the saddest of names: Schreierstoren (Tower of Tears), where weeping women waved farewell to their seafaring men.

Top 10 Bridges

1. Magere Brug (Amstel)
2. Blauwbrug (Amstel)
3. Hogesluis (Amstel)
4. Nieuwe Amstelbrug (Amstel)
5. Berlagebrug (Amstel)
6. Torensluis (Singel)
7. St Antoniessluis (Zwanenburgwal)
8. Seven hump-back bridges (Reguliersgracht)
9. White wooden drawbridges (Western Islands)
10. Sleutelbrug (Oudezijds Voorburgwal)

The Grachtengordel

Amsterdam's magnificent semicircle of three canals – Prinsengracht, Keizersgracht and Herengracht – is the city's defining characteristic. Lined by elegant gabled houses, and connected by intimate cross-streets, it was devised in the early 17th century to cope with the rapid rise in population, and was built in two stages during the century. This costly Plan of Three Canals was purely aesthetic, taking no account of existing waterways. The land along the banks was sold in single plots; the wealthy bought two together so that they could build larger houses.

Amsterdam had its unlikely beginnings some 400 years before, when a fishing settlement grew up on the marshy banks of the river Amstel. (It was dammed in 1222 – hence the name, a contraction of Amstelledamme.) As the town began to expand, canals were cut to drain more land and provide transport channels, and outer canals were fortified. A glance at a map clearly shows the limits of the medieval town, bounded by the curved Singel, with the Grachtengordel fanning out beyond.

Amsterdam's Top 10

Magere Brug
Built in 1672 and so narrow that it was named the Skinny Bridge, this much-loved double-leaf wooden drawbridge was rebuilt in 1969.

Plan of Amsterdam (1648) showing the Grachtengordel

 For details of canal tours **See p136**

11

TOP10 Rijksmuseum

The magnificent national museum of the Netherlands possesses nearly seven million works of art, only a fraction of which is on display. Established by King Louis Napoleon in 1808, the collection was first housed in the Royal Palace on the Dam, moving later to the Trippenhuis on Kloveniersburgwal. In 1865, the architect P J H Cuypers was commissioned to design a new home for the growing collection in the fashionable area near the Vondelpark; the Rijksmuseum opened in 1885.

Façade of the Rijksmuseum

Key

▨	Basement
▨	Ground floor
▨	First floor

🍴 The museum's dull self-service restaurant is by the right-hand front entrance hall. You might prefer to head for Indonesian Sama Sebo, on P. C. Hoofstraat, or Café Americain *(see p101)*.

🕐 Be prepared: this is a difficult museum to get to grips with in a single visit. To make matters worse, in late 2003, the main building will close for restoration, during which the Philips Wing will stay open, showing a selection of works. Until then, works of art are liable to move around.

- Stadhouderskade 42/Hobbemastraat 19
- Map D5
- 020 674 7000
- www.rijksmuseum.nl
- Open 10am–5pm; closed Jan 1. Garden open 10am–5pm Tue–Sat, 1–5pm Sun
- Admission €8.50 (under 19s free); garden free

1 St Elizabeth's Day Flood
Look carefully at this pastoral scene, highlight of the museum's Dutch History collection, and you will see that a tragedy is unfolding. Painted by an unknown artist in 1500, it recalls a disastrous flood of 1421, when some 20 villages were swept away by floodwater.

2 The Night Watch
The museum's most prized possession is *The Military Company of Captain Frans Banning Cocq* – otherwise known as *The Night Watch* (1642), given pride of place at the head of the Gallery of Honour *(see p15)*.

3 The Jewish Bride
In creating one of the most tender double portraits ever painted (1667), Rembrandt depicted – in an unusually free style – an unknown couple in the guise of biblical characters Isaac and Rebecca.

4 The Milkmaid

The sense of realism in this magical painting by Vermeer (c.1658) is conveyed by his mastery of light, colour and perspective. Seen slightly from below against a bare wall, the simple, sturdy girl seems almost tangible – quiet and still, but for the milk flowing from her jug *(left)*.

Bear in mind that from late 2003, the museum will undergo a major and lengthy restoration **See panel above**

Top 10 Works

5 Gallant Conversation

In the 17th century, paintings of everyday scenes, called genre paintings, became very popular. In this one, by Gerard Ter Borch (1655), a scruffy dog, a candle and a bed convey sexual meaning, and the man appears to hold up a coin.

6 The Windmill at Wijk

In this impressive painting (1670) by Jacob van Ruisdael, a calm scene becomes a dramatic picture, full of excitement.

7 Winter Landscape with Skaters

Dutch landscape artist Hendrick Avercamp specialized in winter scenes packed with delightful detail, such as this one painted in 1608. The longer you gaze at it, the more you notice.

8 Delftware

The Rijksmuseum has a superb collection of Delftware, including an astonishing pyramid vase (c. 1700) more than 1 m (3.2 ft) high, with spouts for displaying highly-prized tulips *(right)*.

9 Dolls House of Petronella Oortman

An exquisitely detailed 17th-century miniature Dutch house, belonging not to a child but to an adult.

10 Portrait of Woman in Turkish Costume

Swiss-born Jean-Etienne Liotard was a portrait artist who used pastels with great skill. After a spell living in Istanbul, he dressed as a Turk, and he liked to array his sitters in Turkish costume as well – as in this subtle and delicate painting of 1745.

Gallery Guide

There are three entrances, two at the front, either side of the central driveway which runs under the building, and one in the Philips Wing on Hobbemastraat. At peak visiting times, it's quicker to use this entrance, housing Asiatic Art, European Paintings, Costume and Textiles and temporary exhibitions, then make your way through to the main building. The museum's highlight collections – Dutch Paintings and Dutch 17th-century Sculpture and Decorative Arts – are on the first floor.

For more on Dutch Artists **See pp46-7**

Left, Centre **Works by Edvard Munch and Gerard Ter Borch** Right **Seated Guanyin**

Rijksmuseum Features

1 The Building
The architect P J H Cuypers attracted strong criticism from the Protestant community, who took exception to the building's Neo-Gothic roofs and ornately decorated façade. King William III refused to set foot inside.

2 The Garden
A little-known, immaculate haven, it is studded with statues and architectural curiosities.

3 Dutch History
The museum's collection includes a chronological display of artifacts tracing the history of the Netherlands. Highlights include *St Elizabeth's Day Flood* (see p12) and *The Battle of Waterloo* by Jan Willem Pieneman.

4 Dutch Paintings
Walk through the Gallery of Honour to survey *The Night Watch*, then begin the tour proper with paintings of the Middle Ages (Room 201). The museum's core is its astonishing array of 17th-century Dutch art, in which every important Dutch artist is represented by a selection of his greatest works. Move on to the 18th- and 19th-century collections, including a Van Gogh self-portrait.

Museum Floorplan

5 European Paintings
Veronese and Goya are among the Italian and Spanish masters represented here. A collection of pastels is displayed separately.

6 Sculpture and Decorative Arts
Highlights include Delftware, dolls houses *(see p13)*, glassware and furniture, as well as the remarkable Chinese Room from Leeuwarden.

7 Costumes and Textiles
Magnificent costumes and textiles, mostly 18th- and 19th-century, are displayed in temporary, themed exhibitions.

8 Asiatic Art
Here, the fruits of Dutch association with the Orient are on display – including beautiful works of art from India, Indonesia, China and Japan.

9 Print Room
The museum owns almost a million works on paper – a small selection is shown in temporary exhibitions in the Print Room on the ground floor.

10 ARIA
The ARIA computer system offers information on 1,250 items from the collection, and helps you to design your own route around the museum.

Top 10 Events in Rembrandt's Life

1. Born in Leiden (1606)
2. Studies with Pieter Lastman (1624)
3. Receives first important commission and marries Saskia van Uylenburgh (1634)
4. Reputation grows; buys large house in Amsterdam (1639) – now the Museum het Rembrandthuis
5. Titus, his only child to survive into adulthood, is born (1641)
6. Saskia dies; The Night Watch completed (1642)
7. Hendrickje Stoffels moves in (1649)
8. Applies for bankruptcy (1656)
9. Titus and Hendrickje acquire the rights to his work
10. Death of Titus (1668); in October of the following year, Rembrandt dies

Rembrandt and *The Night Watch*

Popular belief holds Rembrandt's greatest painting, The Night Watch (1642), responsible for his change in fortune from rich man to pauper. In fact, it was more a case of poor financial management than of public dissatisfaction with the artist, although it's very likely that the militiamen who commissioned the portrait would have been dismayed at the result. The Night Watch differs radically from other contemporary portraits of companies of civic guards, in which they are depicted seated, serious and soberly dressed (see p26). Rembrandt, by contrast, shows a tumultuous scene – the captain issuing orders to his lieutenant, the men taking up arms ready to march. This huge painting was originally even larger, but it was drastically cut down in 1715, when it was moved to the town hall, and the other pieces were lost. In 1975 it was slashed, but repaired.

Self-Portrait as St Paul
Rembrandt's series of self-portraits, painted throughout his life, provide an extraordinary insight into his character.

The Military Company of Captain Frans Banning Cocq – better known as *The Night Watch*

15

⑩ Van Gogh Museum

The most comprehensive collection in the world of Van Gogh's work was amassed by his art dealer brother Theo, and is housed in this museum. It includes more than 200 of his paintings, 580 drawings and hundreds of letters, as well as his Japanese prints and works by contemporaries – though not all are on permanent display. Gerrit Rietveld's airy building, opened in 1973, sets off the paintings to perfection. The display follows Van Gogh's development from the murky peasant scenes of the early 1880s to the anguished final works. An ellipse-shaped extension designed by Kisho Kurokawa was added to the museum in 1999.

Van Gogh Museum façade

🍽 The museum has a useful self-service café, situated on the ground floor.

🕐 To avoid the crowds, arrive at opening time. Stick to the chronological order of the display, and read the excellent English labels.

- Paulus Potterstraat 7
- Map C6
- 020 570 5200
- www.vangogh museum.nl
- Open 10am–6pm daily
- Admission: adults €7; children 13–17 €2.50 (under 13s free)
- Audio tours free; group tours by appointment

1 Sunflowers

This vibrant painting (1889) was intended to be one of a series of still lifes to fill the "Yellow House" at Arles. Van Gogh chose sunflowers because he was expecting Paul Gauguin, and knew his friend liked them. The predominant yellows and oranges contrast with strokes of brilliant mauve and red.

2 The Potato Eaters

The culmination of his years in Nuenen, this was Van Gogh's first major composition (1885). He wanted to portray the peasants realistically, not glamorize them, but the painting was not the critical success he had hoped for.

3 The Courtesan

An interest in Japanese prints inspired Van Gogh to experiment. He copied *The Courtesan* (1887) from a cover of *Paris Illustré*, adding the border of cranes and frogs perhaps in reference to the woman's profession.

Key

Basement

Ground floor

First floor

Second floor

Third floor

4 A Pair of Shoes

Van Gogh gives character to a pair of worn boots in one of the first paintings after his move to Paris (1886). The dark palette harks back to his Nuenen work.

5 Self-Portrait as an Artist

The last and most accomplished in a series of self-portraits painted in 1887, shortly before he left Paris, reveals Van Gogh's distinctive interpretation of Pointillism. He chose himself as subject since he could seldom afford models.

6 Fishing Boats on the Beach at Les Saintes-Maries-de-la-Mer

A trip to the sea in 1888 produced these colourful, stylized boats. Look close and you will see grains of sand, blown on to the canvas and fixed there forever as the paint dried.

8 The Reaper

While undergoing treatment in Saint-Rémy, Van Gogh found solace painting people who worked the land. He painted three versions of The Reaper (1889).

10 Wheatfield with Crows

One of the panoramic landscapes that Van Gogh painted in 1890, during the last days of his life, this famous picture with its dead-end track and menacing, crow-filled sky, perhaps reveals his tortured state of mind.

7 The Bedroom at Arles

The mastery of this painting (1888) lies in the simplicity of the subject and the subtly alternating blocks of colour. Van Gogh was so happy with the result that he made two copies (see p19).

9 Almond Blossom

Van Gogh made this picture of white almond blossom against a blue sky for his new nephew, born in January 1890 and named after him.

Museum Guide

Van Gogh's paintings are displayed by date and place of execution on the first floor of the main building. Works by contemporaries are split between ground and third floor. Exhibitions of drawings and graphic art are staged on the second floor, which also has a study area, where drawings and documents too fragile to be displayed can be viewed. The new wing has three floors, devoted to temporary exhibitions.

For more Amsterdam museums See pp40–41

Left **Van Gogh by Gauguin** Centre **Amsterdam cityscape by Monet** Right **Gauguin self-portrait**

Van Gogh Museum: Other Artists

1 View of Prins Hendrikkade and the Kromme Waal in Amsterdam
Monet painted this cityscape in winter 1874 from a boat on the IJ river.

2 Young Peasant Girl with a Hoe
Jules Breton was an idol of Van Gogh. In rural scenes like this one (1882), he places an idealized figure in a realistic setting.

3 The Veterans
Jean-François Rafaëlli's humble urban scenes were admired by Van Gogh, who knew his work through magazines. He painted *The Veterans* c.1884.

4 The Mountain Sainte-Victoire
Cézanne influenced Van Gogh in his deliberate brushstrokes and his use of light and colour – all evident in this painting of 1885.

5 Young Woman at a Table, "Poudre de Riz"
This early painting by Toulouse-Lautrec (1887), who became a friend of Van Gogh, is probably of his mistress, Suzanne Valadon.

6 Portrait of Bernard's Grandmother
Van Gogh swapped one of his self-portraits for this painting (1887) by Emile Bernard.

Museum Floorplan

7 Portrait of Vincent Van Gogh Painting Sunflowers
Paul Gauguin's picture of his friend was painted in November 1888. Van Gogh felt Gauguin had portrayed him as a madman.

8 Self-Portrait with a Portrait of Bernard, "Les Misérables"
In his powerful self-portrait (1888), Gauguin identified himself with the hero of *Les Misérables*, Jean Valjean.

9 "Grand Paysan"
Jules Dalou shared Van Gogh's preoccupation with peasants, whom he saw as heroic labourers. He devised this life-size sculpture in 1889.

10 Two Women Embracing
Van Gogh's influence on the Dutch artist Jan Sluijters is obvious in the brushwork and colour of this painting of 1906.

Portrait of Bernard's Grandmother

The Life of Vincent Van Gogh

Born on 30 March 1853 in Zundert, Vincent Van Gogh was the eldest son of a pastor and his wife. Aged 16, he joined his uncle's business Goupil & Co., art dealers. Seven years later, displaying increasingly erratic behaviour, he was dismissed. After a couple of false starts as teacher and evangelist, in 1880 he decided to be a painter. From 1883 to 1885, he lived with his parents in Nuenen, but in 1886 he went to Paris to study in Fernand Cormon's studio. He lived with his brother Theo, met renowned artists and changed his style. In 1888, he moved to Arles where he dreamed of establishing an artists' colony with Paul Gauguin. Soon after Gauguin arrived, the friends had a fierce argument, and during a psychotic attack, Van Gogh cut off his own left ear lobe. He enrolled as a voluntary patient in a clinic in Saint-Rémy in 1889. The following year he left for the rural village Auvers-sur-Oise, where his state of mind deteriorated and he shot himself in the chest on 27 July 1890. He died, with Theo at his bedside, two days later.

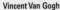
Vincent Van Gogh

Top 10 19th-Century Artists

1. Vincent Van Gogh (1853–1890)
2. Claude Monet (1840–1926)
3. Pierre Auguste Renoir (1841–1919)
4. Paul Cézanne (1839–1906)
5. Auguste Rodin (1840–1917)
6. Edouard Manet (1832–83)
7. Edgar Degas (1834–1917)
8. J M W Turner (1775–1851)
9. Eugène Delacroix (1798–1863)
10. Jean-Baptiste Camille Corot (1796–1875)

The Bedroom at Arles by Van Gogh

Museum Amstelkring

Contrasting sharply with its surroundings in the shabbiest corner of the Red Light District, this lovely 17th-century house has a surprise in store. Concealed in its upper floors is a hidden church, Ons' Lieve Heer op Solder (Our Dear Lord in the Attic), a rare, perfectly preserved example of the many clandestine churches that were built after the Alteration (see facing page). Local Catholics worshipped here from 1663 to 1887, when nearby St Nicolaaskerk was built. Its little-changed interiors transport you back in time to the Dutch Golden Age.

Amstelkring façade with spout gable

For refreshment, head away from the Red Light District to Nieuwmarkt, where In de Waag is an excellent café-restaurant, or to Engelbewaarder in Kloveniersburgwal *(see p50).*

Take one of the free plans and follow the suggested tour of the museum. If you are confused at first, don't worry – all the rooms are clearly marked and you won't miss anything.

- Oudezijds Voorburgwal 40
- Map P2
- 020 624 6604
- www.museum amstelkring.nl
- Open 10am–5pm Mon–Sat, 1–5pm Sun, public hols. Closed 1 Jan, 30 Apr
- Admission: €4.50; concessions €3

Top 10 Features

1. The Building
2. The Front Parlour
3. The Sael
4. The Priest's Room
5. The Clandestine Church
6. The Folding Pulpit
7. The Maria Chapel and Peat Room
8. The Confessional
9. The Rear Houses
10. The Kitchen

The Building
1 The spout-gabled canal house was built in 1661 for Jan Hartman, a Catholic merchant. He combined its attic with the attics of two smaller houses behind to create the hidden church, which was extended in 1735.

The Front Parlour
2 This *(above)* was the merchant's shop, with the wood-floored office behind and a separate entrance for customers. The family and their guests entered though the porch into the dimly-lit marble corridor.

The Sael
3 Adhering to strict rules of proportion and symmetry, the family's formal reception room *(sael)* is a superb example of the Dutch Classical style fashionable in the 17th century *(below)*. It contrasts with the simpler Upstairs Room, which would not have been used to receive guests.

For more on Amsterdam's churches **See pp42–3**

The Priest's Room
4 Formerly the servants' quarters, the Priest's Room is tucked into a corner on a bend in the stairs. It's a tiny, enclosed bedroom with a box bed, simply furnished as it would have been for the priest of the clandestine church, who lived in the house.

Key
▦	Ground floor
▨	First floor
▦	Second floor
▦	Third floor
▦	Fourth floor
▦	Fifth floor

The Clandestine Church
5 At the top of the stairs, the clandestine church *(schuilkerk)* proves a charming and highly unusual sight *(left)*. In 1735 it was remodelled in Baroque style, with the addition of two tiers of galleries, suspended from the roof by cast-iron rods, to provide extra seating.

The Folding Pulpit
6 With space-saving in mind, the ingenious pulpit was designed to fold away under the left column of the altar when not in use. The altar painting is *The Baptism of Christ* by Jacob de Wit (1695–1754).

The Maria Chapel and Peat Room
7 The congregation kept warm with footwarmers fuelled by peat stored in this room above the Maria chapel, which now houses the church's silver.

The Confessional
8 In 1739, this living room in the middle of the three houses became the church's confessional. One of the two wooden confessional boxes still remains *(right)*.

The Rear Houses
9 The rear houses were gradually taken over by the church, but there are still signs of their original use as family rooms.

The Kitchen
10 Once part of the sacristan's secret living quarters, the charming 19th-century kitchen *(left)* has Delft wall tiles, an open hearth, stone sink and black-and-white floor.

The Alteration
The revolt of the (Calvinist) Northern Netherlands against the (Catholic) Spanish Habsburgs began in 1568, but Amsterdam did not decide where its loyalties lay until 1578, when the city joined William of Orange in a peaceful revolution known as the Alteration. Calvinists seized power and Amsterdam became the Protestant capital of an infant Dutch republic. Catholics were no longer allowed to worship in public, but Dutch tolerance ensured that they were able to continue in private.

For more on the Dutch Golden Age **See p27**

TOP 10 Begijnhof

Away from the bustle of the city, this bewitching sanctuary of elegant houses around a tranquil green was founded in 1346 for the members of a lay Catholic sisterhood, the Beguines, the last of whom died in 1971. Although none of the original buildings survive – nor the early design in which the courtyard was surrounded by water – there is a fascinating example of a 15th-century wooden house, a lovely church of the same period, and an appealing hidden chapel. Visitors are asked to respect the privacy of the current residents.

The elegant houses of the Begijnhof

Trendy Café Esprit and traditional Café Hoppe are just round the corner in Spui (at Nos 10 and 18 respectively).

Services are held in Dutch (daily) and French (Sundays) in the Roman Catholic Begijnhof Chapel. Services in English are held in the Protestant Engelse Kerk (Sundays).

In summer, go to a lunchtime concert at the Engelse Kerk.

Pick up an information booklet from Het Houten Huis.

- Spui
- Map M4
- 020 622 1918
- www.begijnhof amsterdam.nl
- Open 9am–5pm daily; Begijnhof Chapel open 1–6:30pm Mon, 9am–6:30pm Tue–Fri, 9am–6pm Sat & Sun
- Free

Top 10 Features

1. Engelse Kerk
2. Begijnhof Chapel
3. Het Houten Huis
4. Courtyard with Wall Plaques
5. Mother Superior's House
6. 17th- and 18th-Century Houses
7. Statue of a Beguine
8. The Beguine in the Gutter
9. Wall Plaque on No. 19
10. Spui Entrance

1 Engelse Kerk

Before the Alteration (see p21), the Beguines worshipped in this pretty 15th-century church (below). Confiscated in 1578, it was let in 1607 to a group of English and Scottish Presbyterians, who renamed it.

2 Begijnhof Chapel

The city's first clandestine chapel was created in 1665, when the Beguines converted two ordinary houses into a little church (see pp20–21). The Miracle of Amsterdam (see p38) is commemorated here.

3 Het Houten Huis

No. 34, Het Houten Huis, is the oldest house in Amsterdam (below), and one of only two wood-fronted houses in the city. It predates the 1521 ban on the construction of wooden houses, introduced to reduce the risk of fire.

4 Courtyard with Wall Plaques

Set into the wall of the courtyard behind Het Houten Huis is a remarkable collection of wall plaques salvaged from demolished houses. In keeping with the religious nature of the Beguines, each one tells a Biblical story.

5 Mother Superior's House

The grandest house, No. 26, belonged to the Mother Superior *(above)*. In the 20th century, the last of the Beguines lived together here.

Plan of the Begijnhof

6 17th- and 18th-Century Houses

After several devastating fires, most of the existing houses were built in the 17th and 18th centuries. They are typically tall and narrow, with large sash windows and spout or neck gables. They were the property of the sisterhood, so if a Beguine left or died, outsiders could not claim her house. Today they provide homes for 100 or so single women.

7 Statue of a Beguine

The statue shows a Beguine dressed in her traditional *falie* (headdress) and long garment of undyed cloth.

8 The Beguine in the Gutter

To make amends for her family's conversion to Protestantism, Cornelia Arens requested in her will not to be buried in the church, but in the gutter outside. Her coffin was left inside the church on 2 May 1654, but the following day it had miraculously moved outside, where she was eventually buried. A plaque marks the spot.

9 Wall Plaque on No. 19

This handsome plaque *(above)* illustrates the return from Egypt to Israel of Jesus, Mary and Joseph after the death of Herod.

10 Spui Entrance

Members of the public use the arched entrance from Gedempte Begijnensloot, but be sure to peep discreetly into the pretty vaulted and tiled passageway leading to Spui.

The Welfare System

Charity lies at the heart of Amsterdam's long tradition of caring for the poor and needy, which goes back to the Middle Ages and continues to the present day. In the 14th century, primary responsibility for social welfare passed from the church to the city authorities. They distributed food to the poor, and set up institutions to care for orphans, the sick and the insane. In the 17th century, a number of wealthy merchants funded almshouses – *hofjes* – providing subsidized mass housing. Some of these *hofjes* are still used for their original purpose today.

For more on hofjes See p92

23

🔟 Amsterdams Historisch Museum

The Historical Museum houses the city's most fascinating collection of artifacts archaeological finds, clothes, jewellery, maps, paintings and sculptures. Originally a convent, in 1580 it became the city orphanage. Handsome extensions were added by Hendrick and Pieter de Keyser before Jacob van Campen's magnificent rebuilding of 1634. The orphans moved out in 1960, and in 197. the museum moved in. Its stunningly presented exhibits and interactive displays chart Amsterdam's growth and metamorphosis over the centuries.

Kalverstraat entrance, 1581

🔲 The David & Goliath café is inside Joost Bilhamer's Kalverstraat entrance.

⭕ Start your sightseeing here; it will help you understand the city when you begin to explore.

The electronic map in Room 1 traces Amsterdam's development from AD 1000 to 2000.

Don't miss the delightful façade stones set into the wall of the museum in St Luciënsteeg.

• Kalverstraat 92;
Sint Luciensteeg 27;
Nieuwezijds Voorburgwal 357
• Map M4
• 020 523 1822
• www.ahm.nl
• Open 10am–5pm Mon–Fri, 11am–5pm Sat, Sun and hols. Closed 1 Jan, 30 Apr, 25 Dec
• Admission: adults €6; children 6–16 €3 (under 6s free); concessions €4.50

Top 10 Works

1. Bird's-eye View of Amsterdam
2. The Return from the Second Voyage to the East Indies
3. Terrestrial and Celestial Globes
4. 19th-century Jewellery Collection
5. Dam Square
6. Turbo Shell
7. Orphan Girls going to Church
8. Dr FM Wibaut (bronze head)
9. The Anatomy Lesson of Dr Jan Deijman
10. Model of the Oosterdok

1 Bird's-eye View of Amsterdam
Cornelis Anthonisz's 1538 map of Amsterdam (the oldest extant) includes the Dam, Oude Kerk and Nieuwe Kerk.

2 The Return from the Second Voyage to the East Indies
Hendrik Corneliszoon Broom's painting (1591) celebrates the first successful expedition to the Far East to buy spices.

3 Terrestrial and Celestial Globes

A pair of costly globes lent prestige to any self-respecting 17th-century intellectual. Joan Willemsz Blaeu must have made this unique pair after 1644 because they show the Australian coast, just discovered by Abel Tasman *(see p39)*.

5 Dam Square

George Hendrik Breitner based his cityscapes on photographs; despite its Impressionist style, this famous painting (1895–98) still has a photographic quality.

Key

- Ground floor
- First floor
- Second floor

7 Orphan Girls going to Church

Nicolaas van der Waaij's charming painting of around 1895 hangs in the anteroom to the Regents' Chamber.

9 The Anatomy Lesson of Dr Jan Deijman

In Rembrandt's original, eight surgeons watched Dr Deijman dissect a corpse. Fire destroyed most of the painting in 1723, but the frontal perspective of the remaining group is still quite remarkable.

10 Model of the Oosterdok

This wonderful model of the Oosterdok Lock dates from 1831, the year work started on the lock itself. It was part of a larger project to counteract a build-up of silt, which barred large ships from the harbour.

6 Turbo Shell

This exquisite mother-of-pearl turbo *marmoratus* is covered in tiny engraved animals. It dates from around 1650 and was probably brought from the Orient by the Dutch East India Company (VOC).

4 19th-century Jewellery

Sophia Lopez Suasso-de Bruijn was a passionate collector of jewellery; even on her deathbed, she spent 5,400 guilders on watches and snuff-boxes. Most of the stunning pieces on display are Italian.

8 Dr F M Wibaut

This powerful bronze head was made in 1934 by Tjipke Visser, favourite sculptor of the Social Democratic Workers' Party (SDAP). The subject was Floor Wibaut, SDAP Councillor for housing in the 1920s, who dedicated himself to building new apartments for the working class.

Museum Guide

The permanent exhibition is arranged on three floors; the "Young City: 1350–1550" is on the ground floor; the "Mighty City: 1550–1815" is split between ground and first floors; the "Modern City: 1815–2000" is split between first and second. A temporary exhibition room and the Civic Guards Gallery are inside the Kalverstraat entrance to the left. The door into the Regents' Chamber is opposite the ticket desk. There is wheelchair access at the St Luciënsteeg entrance.

For more Amsterdam museums **See pp40–41**

Left **Dam Square with the New Town Hall under Construction** Right **Civic Guard**

Historisch Museum Rooms

1 Civic Guards' Gallery

These 16th- and 17th-century group portraits of the Civic Guard are arguably the highlight of the museum (entrance free).

2 Regents' Chamber

The orphanage governors met in this 17th-century room, sympathetically restored in Old Holland style.

3 Room 2: Walking through the City

Aptly named, this room includes a superb collection of 14th- and 15th-century leather shoes, well preserved after centuries in mud.

4 Room 4: Turbulent Times

Displays from the late 16th century include the Civic Guard's Italian-made armour, and silver that escaped melting down for "crisis coins" in 1578.

5 Room 6: The Dam

The bustling heart of the city was a popular subject in 17th-century paintings like Lingelbach's *Dam Square with the New Town Hall under Construction*.

6 Room 9: Social Care, Stern Discipline

In 1613, the city appointed six Almoners with responsibility for the poor and needy. The paintings in this room show them at work.

Museum Floorplan

7 Room 12: The 18th Century

The 18th century saw the decline of Amsterdam and, ultimately, the Republic's defeat by the French. Highlights include *The Arrival of Napoleon at Dam Square* by van Bree.

8 Room 15: 19th-century Cabinet

There was a 19th-century trend for rich industrialists to collect art: old masters as well as contemporary works. These important collections helped establish the public ownership of art.

9 Room 22: Amsterdam 1940–1945

A room devoted to memorabilia of the German occupation.

10 Room 24: Café 't Mandje

A meticulous reconstruction of leather-clad motorbiker Bet van Beeren's famous café on Zeedijk – the first where homosexuals could be open.

Café 't Mandje

Top 10 Highlights of the Golden Age

1. *The Night Watch* by Rembrandt (1642, Rijksmuseum)) *(see p15)*
2. The Grachtengordel, designed by Hendrick Staets (begun in 1613) *(see p11)*
3. Museum Amstelkring (1663) *(see pp20–21)*
4. Westerkerk by Hendrick de Keyser (1631) *(see p91)*
5. Huis met de Hoofden, sometimes attributed to Pieter de Keyser (1622) *(see p91)*
6. Claes Claeszhofje (1616)
7. Silver Marriage Cup by Gerrit Valck (1634) *(right)*
8. Café Hoppe (c.1670) *(see p50)*
9. Delftware (second half 17th century)
10. Orrery of Jan van den Dam (1750, Nederlands Scheepvaart Museum) *(see p123)*

The Golden Age

The economic boom of the 17th century laid the foundations for the flowering of the arts in Amsterdam. Plans were laid to surround the city with a triple ring of canals lined with fine houses, a project which required the work of many architects. The most powerful city in the Dutch Republic recognized the importance of the arts, and rewarded its artists well – and with the supremacy of the Protestants came the freedom to paint secular subjects. To show their wealth and status, rich patrons commissioned portraits of themselves and their families. The artists' best clients, however, were the municipal bodies such as the guilds, who commissioned group portraits, as well as decorative pieces of silver and glass. Painters began to focus their energies on a single area of painting – whether historical, portraiture, interiors, genre, still lives, urban scenes, landscapes or seascapes – and this specialization greatly enhanced the quality of their workmanship.

Silver Marriage Cup
The hinged bowl above the woman's head forms one cup, her full skirt a second. Once the wedding was in full swing, bride and groom would down both together.

Dutch Battle Ships by Ludolf Backhuysen

For more Amsterdam museums **See pp40–41**

27

Oude Kerk

The city's oldest monument and first parish church stands on the site of an early 13th-century wooden chapel that was destroyed by fire. Rebuilt as a small stone hall church in the 14th century, over the years it expanded into a mighty Gothic basilica, now in the heart of the Red Light District (see p77). The interior is stark, stripped of its Catholic treasures during the Iconoclasm of 1566, but it boasts some exquisite stained glass, rare ceiling paintings and a world-famous organ. It is dedicated to St Nicholas, patron saint of the city.

Exterior of the Oude Kerk

🍴 For food and people-watching, head for Nieuwmarkt; In de Waag (Nieuwmarkt 4) is recommended.

🕐 Go to the Dutch Reformed Church service at 11am on Sundays, one of the Spring or Summer concerts, or the World Press Photo exhibition (late April to early June).

Tours of the tower are expensive, so try to make up a group. Bring a pair of binoculars to study the ceiling decoration.

- Oudekerksplein 23
- Map P2
- 020 625 8284
- www.oudekerk.nl
- Open 11am–5pm Mon–Sat, 1–5pm Sun. Closed 1 Jan, 25 Dec, 30 Apr
- Admission €3.80; concessions €3 (separate charge for exhibitions)
- Guided tours by appointment; Tower tours by appointment (phone 020 689 2565)

Top 10 Features

1. Great Organ
2. Maria Kapel
3. Ceiling
4. Saskia's Grave
5. Red Door into the Old Sacristy
6. Decorated Pillars
7. Misericords
8. Spire
9. Stained Glass of the Burgemeesters
10. Little Organ

Great Organ
With its eight pairs of bellows, magnificent oak-encased pipework, marbled wood statues and gilded carving, the great organ is a glorious sight *(right)*. Built by Christian Väter in 1724 and renovated by Johann Caspar Müller 14 years later, it is known as the Väter-Müller organ.

Maria Kapel
The most stunning stained glass is in the three windows of the Lady Chapel. All date from the 16th century; two show scenes from the Virgin's life, above the customary picture of the family who donated the window.

Ceiling
The massive wooden vaulted ceiling is claimed to be the largest in Western Europe, but it was only during restoration work in 1955 that the beautiful 15th-century paintings were revealed.

Saskia's Grave
Among the great and the good buried here is Saskia van Uylenburgh, Rembrandt's first wife, who died in 1642. Her grave is number 29K in the Weitkopers Kapel.

5 Red Door into the Old Sacristy

Rembrandt passed through this door to announce his marriage. "Marry in haste, repent at leisure" is inscribed above it.

Plan of the Oude Kerk

6 Decorated Pillars

Relics of the period before 1578, these pillars once supported niches for statues of the Apostles destroyed in the Iconoclasm, and were painted to look like brocade, since the real thing was too expensive, and unsuited to the humid atmosphere.

7 Misericords

The 15th-century misericords helped choristers take the weight off their feet (left). They are decorated with charming carvings illustrating traditional Dutch proverbs.

8 Spire

From the graceful late-Gothic spire, built by Joost Bilhamer in 1565, there are splendid views over the Oude Zijde. The tower contains a 47-bell carillon, a 17th-century addition which rings out every Saturday afternoon.

9 Stained Glass of the Burgemeesters

The colourful stained glass windows flanking the chancel depict the arms of the city burgomasters from 1578 to 1807 (left). One was designed by De Angeli in 1758; the other by Pieter Jansz in 1654.

10 Little Organ

Attractively painted shutters form the original casing (1658) – however, the pipework was replaced in 1965. Tuned as it would have been before 1700, early music can now be part of the repertoire.

The Iconoclasm of 1566

In the 1566 Iconoclasm, or *Beeldenstorm* – precursor to the Alteration of 1578 (see p21) when the city became Protestant – the Calvinists looted Catholic churches and destroyed their treasures, among them the Oude Kerk's pictures, altars and statues. Only the ceiling paintings and stained glass were spared, as they were out of reach. The Calvinists also disapproved of the beggars and pedlars who gathered in the church, and threw them out, ending its role as a city meeting place.

For more Amsterdam churches See pp42–3

ᵀᴼᴾ10 Museum Van Loon

Step back into the 18th century at this delightful canal house on Keizersgracht, which has been the property of the prestigious Van Loon family (co-founders of the Dutch East India Company, later bankers and royal courtiers) since 1884. In the 1970s, the family opened it to the public, having painstakingly restored it to its appearance in the 1750s, when it was owned by Dr Abraham van Hagen and his heiress wife Catharina Trip. It is beautifully furnished with Van Loon family possessions throughout.

Façade of the Museum Van Loon

🍽 There is no café; head for nearby Nieuwe Spiegelstraat or Utrechtsestraat for a good choice.

🌀 Serene and elegant, the Museum Van Loon makes a perfect visit for adults, but is not so well suited to young children.

• Keizersgracht 672
• Map E5
• 020 624 5255
• www.museum vanloon.nl
• Open 11am–5pm Fri–Mon, Tue–Thu by appointment
• Admission €4.50; concessions €3
• Guided tours on request

Top 10 Features

1. The Building
2. The Staircase
3. The Family Portraits
4. The Wedding Portrait
5. The Garden
6. The Dining Service
7. The Gold Coin Collection
8. The Painted Room
9. The Romantic Double Portrait
10. The Kitchen

The Building

1 In 1672, Jeremias van Raey built two large houses on Keizersgracht. One he occupied himself, the other – No. 672, now the Museum Van Loon – he rented to Rembrandt's most famous pupil, Ferdinand Bol.

The Staircase

2 The balustrade was installed by Dr Van Hagen, who had his and his wife's names incorporated into the ornate brass work. When the canals ceased to freeze over regularly, the 18th-century sledge in the hall found a new use as a plant stand.

The Family Portraits

3 Portraits of the Van Loon family are displayed throughout the house.

The Wedding Portrait

4 Jan Molenaer's first major commission in Amsterdam portrays the whole family. It's a second marriage: the bride holds her stepson's hand in an act of acceptance, while the fallen chair symbolizes the groom's deceased brother.

The Garden

5 Laid out in the 1970s according to a plan of the property of 1700, the peaceful garden ends in the false Neo-Classical façade of the coach house *(below)*. Look carefully and you will see that the upstairs windows are in fact painted, pretty curtains and all.

Key

▨	Ground floor
▨	First floor
▨	Second floor

The Dining Service

6 Rare 18th-century Dutch porcelain and 19th-century Limoges ware grace the dining room.

The Gold Coin Collection

7 Over the centuries, five Van Loon couples have celebrated their golden wedding; each had gold coins specially minted.

The Painted Room

8 Painted wallpapers such as these, featuring ruins, Classical buildings and human figures, were very popular in the 1700s.

The Romantic Double Portrait

9 Painted by J F A Tischbein in 1791, this intimate, relaxed portrait of these Van Loon ancestors is typical of the Age of Enlightenment, conveying love and happiness as well as duty.

The Kitchen

10 Cosy and inviting, the basement kitchen has been recently restored to look as it did in a photograph of 1900.

Museum Guide

Visitors are welcomed as guests in a private house and encouraged to wander around freely. They are allowed to walk on the carpets and nothing is roped off. Temporary exhibitions of modern art and sculpture are often on display in both the house and garden.

🔟 Anne Frankhuis

This deeply moving museum tells a tragic story. When in 1942 the Germans began to round up Jews in Amsterdam, the Frank and Van Pels families went into hiding. For 25 months, they hid in a secret annexe in Otto Frank's business premises on Prinsengracht, now the Anne Frankhuis. In August 1944, they were betrayed and deported. Only Otto survived. The diary of his daughter, Anne, who died in Bergen-Belsen concentration camp in March 1945 at the age of 15, has made her one of the most inspiring figures of the 20th century.

Façade of No. 263 Prinsengracht

🍴 There is a pleasant, airy café, though it is sometimes noisy with school parties.

🕐 Arrive early or late in the day; there are usually long queues.

Be careful as you move round the house: the stairs are steep and narrow.

The visit is a moving experience, so plan something contemplative afterwards: climb the Westerkerk spire, or walk to the Western Islands.

• Prinsengracht 263 (entrance at 267)
• Map L2
• 020 556 7100
• www.annefrank.nl
• Open Sep–Mar: 9am–7pm daily; Apr–Aug: 9am–9pm daily. Closed Yom Kippur
• Admission adults €6.50; children 10–17 €3; children under 10 free
• No disabled access

Top 10 Features

1. The Warehouse
2. The Offices
3. The Moveable Bookcase
4. The Secret Annexe
5. Anne's Room
6. The Chestnut Tree
7. The Front Attic
8. The Diary Room
9. Educational Resources
10. The Exhibition Room

1 The Warehouse
Otto Frank ran a business making pectin for jam, and spice and herb mixtures. The annexe in which the families hid was over his warehouse, so they had to keep quiet for fear that the warehouse workers would hear them.

2 The Offices
Visitors continue upstairs to the offices of Otto Frank and the staff who helped to hide him and his family, along with Otto's business partner, Hermann Van Pels, and his wife and son. In Anne's diary, the Van Pels became the Van Daans.

3 The Moveable Bookcase
To camouflage the entrance to the annexe, one of the helpers made a swinging bookcase. As Anne wrote, "no one could ever suspect that there could be so many rooms hidden behind..."

4 The Secret Annexe
The claustrophobic rooms in which the eight lived have been left unfurnished, as they were when the Germans cleared their possessions after their arrest. On one wall, pencil marks record the growth of Anne and her sister Margot.

5 Anne's Room

After a while, Margot moved in with her parents, and Anne had to share her room with a new member of the group, a dentist called Fritz Pfeffer – in Anne's estimation, "a very nice man". Anne's film-star pin-ups are still up on the wall.

Key to floorplan

- Ground floor
- First floor
- Second floor
- Third floor
- Attic

8, 9 and 10 *in separate building*

6 The Chestnut Tree

Some years ago, when this tree was dying, the authorities paid a small fortune to have it preserved because it was a favourite of Anne's.

7 The Front Attic

In a moving display, the fate of each member of the group unfolds. Anne and Margot died a month before Bergen-Belsen was liberated.

9 Educational Resources

At the end of the tour, interactive video positions enable you to find out more about various aspects of the story, and the library of press clippings, books and videos is open to everyone.

8 The Diary Room

As well as the now famous red-checked diary, which she kept every day, Anne wrote short stories and ideas for novels. As time went on, she began to edit her original diary with a book called *The Secret Annexe* in mind.

10 The Exhibition Room

The Anne Frank Foundation promotes racial tolerance through education. After the tour, visitors can participate in a video presentation on related issues.

Anne Frank's Diary

On the day the family were taken away, Miep Gies found Anne's diary. With the words "here is your daughter Anne's legacy to you", she handed it to Otto Frank on his return from Auschwitz. He prepared a transcript, and the diary was published to great acclaim in the Netherlands in 1947, and in Britain and the United States in 1952. It has since been published in more than 60 languages. Over 800,000 people visit the museum each year.

For more Jewish sights in Amsterdam **See pp48–9**

🔟 Dam Square

The very heart of Amsterdam, Dam Square – or "the Dam", as the locals call it – marks the site of the original 13th-century dam on the Amstel river (see p11). An architectural parade spanning six centuries includes the glorious Nieuwe Kerk and the Koninklijke Paleis. By the 17th century, with the town hall here and the Exchange nearby, the Dam had become the focus of Amsterdam's political and commercial life. The passage of years may have eroded some of its grandeur – but certainly none of its colour or its vitality.

A horse and trap near the Nationaal Monument

💬 There are cafés in Madame Tussaud's, De Bijenkorf and the Nieuwe Kerk – the latter with a terrace overlooking the Dam.

🕐 Go to one of the concerts, lectures or exhibitions held at the Nieuwe Kerk.

• Map M3, N3
• Koninklijk Paleis: open Feb–Jun & Sep–Nov: 12:30–5pm Tue–Thu; late Jun–mid-Sep: 11am–5pm daily (times may vary). 020 624 8698. Admission: adults €4.50; children 6–16 €3.60; under 6s free
• Nieuwe Kerk: open 10am–6pm daily. 020 638 6909. Free
• Madame Tussaud's Scenerama: Peek & Cloppenburg Building. 020 522 1010. Open Sep–Jun: 10am–5:30pm daily; mid-Jul–Aug: 9:30am–7:30 pm daily. Admission Sep–Jun: adults €12.50, children 5–16 €8.50; Jul–Aug: adults 17–59 €14, over 60s €12, children 5–16 €10; under 5s free

Top 10 Sights

1. Koninklijk Paleis
2. Nieuwe Kerk
3. Nationaal Monument
4. Madame Tussaud's Scenerama
5. Damrak
6. De Bijenkorf
7. Rokin
8. Kalverstraat
9. Grand Hotel Krasnapolsky
10. Street Performances and Events

Koninklijk Paleis
1 Built as the town hall, Jacob van Campen's unsmiling Classical edifice symbolizes the civic power of 17th-century Amsterdam *(above)*. It is still used for state occasions *(see p39)*.

Nieuwe Kerk
2 Now a cultural centre, the Nieuwe Kerk has hosted royal events since 1814. Its treasures include a Jacob van Campen organ and an elaborately carved pulpit by Albert Vinckenbrinck *(see p42)*.

Nationaal Monument
3 This 22 m (70 ft) obelisk commemorates the Dutch killed in World War II *(above & centre)*. Embedded in the wall behind are urns containing soil from the Dutch provinces and colonies.

4 Madame Tussaud's Scenerama
Displays at this outpost of the London waxworks range from the fascinating to the bizarre. Special effects, including animatronics, bring to life scenes from Holland's past.

5 Damrak
Damrak was once the medieval city's busiest canal, with ships sailing up to be unloaded at the Dam. In 1672 the canal was filled in, and Damrak developed into the hectic shopping street it is today.

Plan of Dam Square

6 De Bijenkorf
Amsterdam's best-known department store has a vast perfumery, designer fashion boutiques and much more.

7 Rokin
The Rokin had its heyday in the 19th century, when its broad sweep was a promenade for the well-to-do.

8 Kalverstraat
Music shops jostle for space with tacky clothes stores at the Dam end of this pedestrian shopping street.

9 Grand Hotel Krasnapolsky
Adolf Wilhelm Krasnapolsky, an emigré Polish tailor with ambition, painted the down-at-heel Nieuwe Poolsche Koffiehuis in the 1870s, swiftly transforming it into a fashionable hotel (below).

10 Street Performances and Events
Busking, mime, funfairs, book fairs, exhibitions, concerts – such things have gone on in the Dam since J Cabalt introduced his puppet show in 1900.

Inside the Koninklijk Paleis

The ponderous exterior belies the magnificent interior – especially the dramatic Burgerzaal (Citizen's Chamber). See fine sculptures by Artus Quellien and Rombout Verhulst, ceilings and friezes by Rembrandt's pupils, and Empire furniture of Louis Napoleon. The *Vierschaar* (Tribunal) is a macabre room, still intact, where judges meted out tough – and often terminal – justice.

For more Amsterdam churches See pp42–3

35

Left **The Arrival of Napoleon at Dam Square** Right **German wartime propaganda poster**

Moments in Amsterdam's History

1 c.1125: First Settlers

Fishermen settled at the mouth of the Amstel river, building huts on man-made mounds called *terps* for flood protection. With the growth of the new settlement came feudal conflict between the self-made Counts of Holland and Lords van Amstel.

2 1275: Freedom from Tolls

In the earliest document to refer to Amsterdam, Count Floris V of Holland granted its citizens exemption from tolls when transporting their goods by river across his territory at The Hague.

3 1345: Miracle of Amsterdam

At a house in Kalverstraat, a priest gave a dying man the last sacraments. He was unable to keep down the communion wafer, so it was thrown on the fire. Next morning, the wafer was found intact among the embers. News of the miracle spread, and Amsterdam soon became a place of pilgrimage.

Miracle of Amsterdam

4 1566 and 1578: Iconoclasm and Alteration

As Protestantism swept northern Europe, Dutch Calvinists rebelled against their intolerant Spanish Catholic ruler, Philip II. In the *Beeldenstorm* or Iconoclasm, the Calvinists stormed the Catholic churches and destroyed their religious artifacts. The city finally became Protestant, in a peaceful revolution known as the *Alteratie* or Alteration (see p21).

5 1609: Plans for the Grachtengordel

The dawn of the Golden Age, when the arts flourished in Amsterdam (see p27), saw ambitious plans for a triple canal ring around the city (see p11). Herengracht, Keizersgracht and Prinsengracht were built in two stages, starting in 1613 and 1663.

6 1634–37: Tulipmania

The Dutch passion for tulips dates from the late 16th century, when the first bulbs were imported from Asia. In 1634, the tulip was quoted on the Stock Exchange, and speculation began. Fortunes were made overnight as the craze led to spectacular price increases; the inevitable crash caused scores of bankruptcies.

7 1806: Kingdom of the Netherlands Established

After the formation of the Batavian Republic in 1795, rule was shared between the invading French and the Dutch Patriots. In 1806, Napoleon Bonaparte took over the Republic, created the Kingdom of the Netherlands and installed his brother, Louis Napoleon, as head of state.

8 1940–45: German Occupation

Despite Dutch neutrality, Germany invaded Holland in May 1940. With the deportation of Jews to concentration camps from 1942 onwards, the Dutch Resistance became active and underground newspapers thrived. Canadian troops liberated Amsterdam on 5 May 1945.

9 Mid-1960s: Provo Demonstrations

The radical Provo movement took off in the 1960s, fuelled by antagonism to the city's transport and housing policies. Street demonstrations turned into full-scale rioting on 10 March 1966, the day of Princess Beatrix's wedding to German aristocrat Claus von Amsberg. The Provos won seats on the city council, but their popularity was short-lived.

10 2002: Wedding of the Crown Prince

On 2 February 2002, Crown Prince Willem-Alexander married Máxima Zorreguieta in the Nieuwe Kerk, followed by a reception in the Koninklijke Paleis. After a difficult start, due to her father's involvement with the Videla regime in Argentina, Máxima won the hearts of the Dutch public.

Wedding of the Crown Prince

Top 10 Historic Characters

1 William of Orange
"William the Silent" (1533–84) led the Protestant rebellion against Philip II. He was assassinated.

2 Willem Barentsz
This explorer (1550–97) failed to discover the north-east passage but left behind invaluable maps.

3 Frederik Hendrik
An effective politician, William of Orange's youngest son (1584–1647) became *Stadhouder* in 1625.

4 Pieter Stuyvesant
Stuyvesant (1592–1672) was Governor of the colony of Nieuw Amsterdam, later to be New York, from 1646–64.

5 Abel Tasman
In search of trade routes to South America, Tasman (1603–c.1659) discovered Tasmania and New Zealand.

6 Michiel de Ruyter
This revered Dutch admiral (1607–76) set fire to the English fleet in the Medway in 1667.

7 Jan de Witt
A leading politician in the Anglo-Dutch Wars (1625–72), he was killed by a mob.

8 William III
William (1650–1702) was *Stadhouder* from 1672 until his promotion to King of England in 1688.

9 Louis Napoleon
Brother of Napoleon I, Louis (1778–1846) was King of the Netherlands between 1806 and 1810.

10 Johan Thorbecke
Liberal Prime Minister Johan Rudolf Thorbecke (1798–1872) was architect of the 1848 Constitution.

Left **Rijksmuseum** Right **Nederlands Scheepvaart Museum**

🔟 Museums

1 Rijksmuseum
The world's greatest collection of 17th-century Dutch art is housed in this grand municipal art museum – and there's so much more to see besides *(see pp12–15)*.

2 Van Gogh Museum
The permanent home for hundreds of works by this troubled artist also displays work by his contemporaries *(see pp16–19)*.

3 Amsterdams Historisch Museum
First a convent, then the city orphanage, now a wonderful museum charting the history of Amsterdam and, in particular, its meteoric rise during the Golden Age *(see pp24–7)*.

Stedelijk Museum

4 Museum Amstelkring
The 17th-century domestic interiors would be fascinating in themselves, but the astonishing thing about this historic canal house is the secret Catholic church hidden on its upper floors *(see pp20–1)*.

5 Stedelijk Museum
At time of writing, the national museum of modern art, in its specially designed building by A W Weissman, is closed for major renovation work – it is due to reopen in 2005. Until then, part of its dynamic collection, which includes works by Matisse, Chagall, Picasso, Mondriaan, de Kooning and Gerrit Rietveld, will be displayed in temporary exhibitions at a variety of locations around Amsterdam *(see p115)*.

6 Anne Frankhuis
This world-famous yet movingly simple museum is dedicated to the young diarist who hid here from the Nazis with her family *(see pp32–3)*.

7 Museum Van Loon
Another canal-house-turned-museum, the Van Loon recreate high-society life in the 18th century *(see pp30–31)*.

Amsterdams Historisch Museum

8 Museum Willet-Holthuysen

Like the Museum Van Loon, the Willet-Holthuysen affords a rare glimpse inside a grand canal house – and into the lives of the wealthy merchants who lived there. Built in 1685, the interior is decorated in 18th-century style. A mild sense of melancholy pervades the building *(see p107)*.

Museum Het Rembrandthuis

9 Nederlands Scheepvaart Museum

Holding the largest collection of boats in the world, and crammed with fascinating objects, the Nederlands Scheepvaart became a museum in 1973, when the Dutch Navy vacated the building. Solid and four-square, Daniel Stalpaert's imposing classical-style arsenal was built for the Admiralty in 1656 during the Golden Age of Dutch maritime history. Among the museum's treasures are cannons and cutlasses, instruments and maps, figureheads and anchors, paintings and meticulously accurate models *(see p123)*.

10 Museum Het Rembrandthuis

Completely restored to look as it did in Rembrandt's day, this handsome red-shuttered house was the artist's home during his years of prosperity (1639–58). Entering the rooms is a little like stepping into a painting: they are typical Dutch interiors with black-and-white tiled floors, traditional box beds, and paintings by Rembrandt's contemporaries. Perhaps the two most fascinating sights here are the recreation of his studio, and the room – in a new wing – devoted to his magical etchings, many of which show his compassion for the common people: quacksalver, pancake woman, beggars, street musicians. A video about the recent restoration work is shown in the basement *(see p77)*.

Left **Noorderkerk** Right **De Krijtberg**

Väter-Müller organ, Oude Kerk

Zuiderkerk

TOP 10 Churches

1 Oude Kerk
The oldest and greatest of Amsterdam's churches (see pp28-9).

2 Nieuwe Kerk
The second parish church in Amsterdam was built after the congregation outgrew the Oude Kerk. Burnt down several times, its oldest part is the choir, dating from around 1400 (see pp34, 83).

3 Westerkerk
After the Alteration of 1578 (see p21), the first Dutch Protestant churches to be built were the Zuiderkerk, the Noorderkerk and the Westerkerk – all designed by Hendrick de Keyser. The Westerkerk has the city's tallest tower, topped by the gaily painted imperial crown of Maximilian of Austria (see p91).

4 Zuiderkerk
The splendid spire, with its columns, clocks, pinnacles and onion dome, was much admired by Sir Christopher Wren, and is still a prominent city landmark, even though the Zuiderkerk ceased to function as a church in 1929. Today it is an information centre for urban development, surrounded by modern community housing. ◈ Zuiderkerkhof 72 • Map P4 • Church open 11am–4pm Mon, 9am–4pm Tue–Fri, 9am–8pm Thu. Free • Tower open Jun-Sep: 2–4pm Wed–Sat. Admission charge

5 Noorderkerk
Hendrick de Keyser's last church, begun a year before he died in 1621, is quite different in style. Built for the poor of the Jordaan, it is an austere brick building with only the shortest of spires. Designed on a Greek Cross plan, it has a central pulpit and four hipped roofs. ◈ Noordermarkt 44–48 • Map D2 • Open 11am–1pm Sat • Free

6 Engelse Kerk
In the middle of the Begijnhof, the pretty English Reform Church got its name from the English (and Scottish) Presbyterians who worshipped there after it was requisitioned in 1578 (see pp22-3).

De Krijtberg

7 Like many Catholic churches in Amsterdam, De Krijtberg (meaning Chalk Mountain) is known by its nickname rather than its official name, Franciscus Xaveriuskerk (after St Francis Xavier, a founding Jesuit monk); designed in 1884 by Alfred Tepe, it replaced a clandestine Jesuit chapel *(see p21)*. It's an impressive building, with an elegant, twin-steepled Neo-Gothic façade and an ornate interior that stands in marked contrast to the austerity of the city's Protestant churches. ◈ *Singel 448 • Map M5 • Open 30 mins before services: 12:30pm & 5:45pm Mon–Fri; 12:30pm & 5:15pm Sat; 9:30am, 11am, 12:30pm & 5:15pm Sun Free*

Mozes en Aäronkerk

8 Here, the nickname comes from two gablestones depicting Moses and Aäron on the house fronts that hid a clandestine church within. It was replaced in 1841 by the present Neo-Classical building, its towers inspired by St Sulpice in Paris. *Waterlooplein 205 • Map Q5*

St Nicolaaskerk

9 Dedicated to the patron saint of sea-farers, the church was commissioned by the congregation of *Ons' Lieve Heer op Solder (see pp20–21)*. A C Bleys, the architect, came up with a Neo-Renaissance building of a somewhat grim and forbidding character. ◈ *Prins Hendrikkade 76 • Map Q1 Open Apr–Oct: 9:30am–5:30pm • Free*

St Nicolaas Kerk

Waalse Kerk

10 This church – founded in 1409 – is all that is left of the convent of St Paul. Its name means Walloon Church, a reference to the Low Countries (now Belgium), from where Huguenots fled the Catholic terror to seek refuge in Amsterdam. In 1586 they were given use of the Waalse Kerk so that they could continue their worship in French. It has a historic organ dating from 1680, renovated in 1734 by master organ builder Christian Müller. ◈ *Walenpleintje 159 • Map P4*

Left **Paleis van Justitie** Right **Greenpeace Building**

🏛10 Historic Buildings

1 Schreierstoren
The Schreierstoren (Tower of Tears) is one of Amsterdam's oldest buildings *(see p10)* – a surviving fragment of the medieval city wall. ◈ *Prins Hendrikkade 94–5 • Map Q2*

2 In't Aepjen
One of two remaining wood-fronted houses in Amsterdam *(see p22)*, In't Aepjen was built in 1550 as a sailors' hostel, and is now a bar. The name means "In the monkeys": when sailors couldn't pay their bills, they would barter – sometimes with pet monkeys, which were popular in those days. ◈ *Zeedijk 1 • Map P2*

3 Oostindisch Huis
Seen from the courtyard, the impressive red-brick façade, with its ornate entrance and stone-dressed windows, was the height of corporate fashion. Headquarters of the once might Dutch East India Company (VOC it was built in 1605, probably by Hendrick de Keyser, and is now part of Amsterdam University. ◈ *Oude Hoogstraat 24 • Map P4*

4 De Gooyer Windmill
If you are lucky, you might see the vast, streamlined sails of thi 18th-century corn mill creak into motion. Buil in 1725, the whole octagonal structure wa painstakingly moved to its present site in 1814 ◈ *Funenkade 5 • Map H4*

De Gooyer Windmill

5 Pintohuis
Now a public library, the Pintohuis is named after the Portuguese merchant Isaac de Pinto, who paid an exorbitant 30,000 guilders for it in 1651. ◈ *Sint Antoniesbreestraat 6 • Map Q4 • 020 624 3184 • Open 2–8pm Mon & Wed, 2–5pm Fri, 11am–2pm Sat; closed Sat in Jul*

6 Trippenhuis
Justus Vingboons' grandiose façade with false middle window (1662) concealed the two separat homes of the powerful Trip brothers – arms dealers, hence the pair of chimneys resembling cannons. The tiny house at No. 26 was built for their coachman. ◈ *Kloveniersburgwal 29 • Map P4*

Schreierstoren

Scheepvaarthuis

7 Westindisch Huis

The city of New York was conceived in the Dutch West India Company building, and Pieter Stuyvesant's statue still surveys the courtyard *(see p39)*. Built in 1615, its classical proportions belie its origins as a meat market. ❧ *Haarlemmerstraat 75 • Map D2*

8 Paleis van Justitie

This sober, monumental building in Empire style is a conversion of the Almoners' Orphanage by city architect Jan de Greef. ❧ *Prinsengracht 434–6 • Map K6*

9 Greenpeace Building

Gerrit van Arkel's eye-catching 1905 building is a fine example of *Nieuwe Kunst*, the Dutch version of Art Nouveau. Built for an insurance company, it is now the world headquarters of the environmental campaigner Greenpeace. ❧ *Keizersgracht 174–6 • Map L2*

10 Scheepvaarthuis

Designed as shipping company offices by van der Mey, de Klerk and Kramer, this fanciful building (1916) is smothered in nautical whimsy – mariners, monsters, and mermaids. ❧ *Prins Hendrikkade 108 • Map Q2*

Top 10 Architectural Features

1 Triangular Gable

This simple triangular-shaped gable can be seen on Het Houten Huis *(see p22)*.

2 Bell Gable

Fashionable in the late 17th and 18th centuries, bell-shaped gables can be flamboyant (Prinsengracht 126) or unadorned (Leliegracht 57).

3 Neck Gable

Made popular by Philips Vingboons, this gable has a raised centrepiece; Oude Turfmarkt 145 is an example.

4 Spout Gable

This plain triangular gable topped by a spout was used for warehouses, like those at Entrepotdok *(see p123)*.

5 Step Gable

Common from 1600 to 1665, this gable has steps on both sides: Huis op de drie Grachten has three *(see p79)*.

6 Wall Plaque

Before numbering was introduced, houses were identified by plaques *(see p23)*.

7 Claw Piece

Sculptures – frequently of dolphins – were made to fill the right angles of gables, as in Oudezijds Voorburgwal 119.

8 Mask

This type of Renaissance decoration depicts a human or animal face, and can be seen at Oudezijds Voorburgwal 57.

9 Cornices

From 1690, gables fell out of vogue and decorative top mouldings came in: examples line the Herengracht.

10 Pediment Carvings

Carvings often decorate the triangular or rounded form above doorways: see the Felix Meritis Building *(see p57)*.

Left *Allegory of Painting* by Vermeer Right *Wheatfield with Crows* by Van Gogh

Dutch Artists

1 Jan Van Scorel
After prolonged stays in Germany, Venice and Rome, where he studied the works of Giorgione, Michelangelo and Raphael, Jan Van Scorel (1495–1562) returned to Utrecht in 1524. He introduced the techniques of the Renaissance to the Northern Netherlands; his portraits fuse Italian solidity of form with Netherlandish delicacy.

2 Rembrandt van Rijn
The greatest artist of the Dutch Golden Age *(see p15)*.

3 Frans Hals
Much loved for his technique of capturing character and fleeting expression in his sitters, Frans Hals (1580–1666) brought a new realism to portraiture in the 17th century. His fine group portraits of civic guards are displayed in the Frans Hals Museum in Haarlem *(see p72)*.

4 Johannes Vermeer
Relatively little is known about the life of this sublime Delft artist (1632–75), who inherited his father's art-dealing business and painted purely for pleasure. He gained some recognition in Holland during his lifetime, but his importance was not established until the late 19th century, and rests on less than 40 known works – mainly domestic interiors with figures – that are extraordinary in their handling of space, light and colour. He was married with 11 children. On his death, his wife was declared bankrupt, and his baker kept two of his paintings against unpaid bills.

Self Portrait at a Young Age by Rembrandt

5 Jan Steen
A prolific painter of the genre (everyday) scenes so popular in the Dutch 17th century, Jan Steen (1625–79) was an innkeeper as well as an artist. His often bawdy tavern and household narratives were packed with hidden messages (red stockings for prostitution, oysters for sexual liaison, broken eggshells for mortality), creating allegories with a moral purpose.

6 Jacob van Ruisdael
Born in Haarlem, Jacob van Ruisdael (1629–1682), though not highly regarded in his own day, has come to be seen as one of the finest landscape and seascape painters of the Dutch school. His works are filled with restless skies and naturalistic details. Even calm scenes such as *The Windmill at Wijk* have a sense of dramatic grandeur.

 For more on Dutch paintings **See pp12–19**

7 Pieter Claesz

As well as portraits, genre paintings and landscapes, still lives had an important place in Dutch 17th-century art. Peter Claesz (1597–1661) reached a peak of technical skill in his harmonious if academic compositions, which are replete with symbolic detail.

8 Vincent Van Gogh

A troubled genius who left a vast body of work, despite his tragically short life *(see p19)*.

9 Piet Mondriaan

Although he lived in London, Paris and New York (and few of his works are on show in Amsterdam), Mondriaan was born and grew up in Holland (1872–1944). A leading member of the De Stijl movement, he created an abstract style using the simplest elements: straight lines and blocks of primary colour, arranged on the canvas to create harmony and balance.

10 Karel Appel

Born in 1921, Karel Appel was one of the founders of the Cobra movement, started in 1948, which combined expressionist, abstract and surrealist influences *(see p128)*. His colourful works display a savage, forceful directness combined with an almost childlike optimism. "I paint like a barbarian in a barbarous age", he said.

Children with Dog by Karel Appel

Top 10 Dutch Literary Figures

1 Desiderius Erasmus
Scholar and humanist (1466–1536). Friend of Thomas More, no friend of Luther.

2 Hugo Grotius
Statesman and philosopher (1583–1645). Author of *De Jure Belli et Pacis*, the foundation stone of international law.

3 Gerbrant Bredero
Satirical poet and play-wright (1585–1618), best known for *De Spaanse Brabander*.

4 Joost van den Vondel
Important playwright and poet (1586–1679) famed for his ornate style. Author of *Gijsbrecht van Amstel*.

5 Jan Six
Poet, playwright (1618–1700) and friend of Rembrandt, who painted his portrait.

6 Baruch Spinoza
Philosopher (1632–77) expelled by Amsterdam's Jewish community for his secular beliefs.

7 Multatuli
Pen name of Eduard Douwes Dekker (1820–87), whose work in colonial Java inspired his best-known novel *Max Havelaar*.

8 Anne Frank
Teenage victim (1929–44) of the Holocaust. Her eloquent diary has sold in its millions.

9 Gerard Reve
Novelist (b.1923) strongly influenced by his Catholicism and his homosexuality.

10 Cees Nooteboom
Prolific man of letters (b.1933) whose fiction is at best observant and poignant, at worst experimental and elusive.

Left **Joods Historisch Museum** Right **Jodenbuurt**

Jewish Sights

1 Anne Frankhuis
The plight of Jews like the Franks, forced into hiding by the Nazis, was brought to light by Anne's poignant diary; the house where they hid for 25 months is now a museum *(see pp32–3)*.

2 Joods Historisch Museum
This remarkable museum represents all aspects of Judaism and the history and culture of the Jews who settled in the Netherlands. On show are some marvellous paintings by Jewish artists, fascinating displays about the diamond industry, and exhibits that bring home the true horror of the Holocaust *(see p78)*.

3 Portugees-Israëlitische Synagoge
Inspired by the Temple of Solomon in Jerusalem, Elias Bouman's bulky red-brick synagogue is still the core of the small Sephardic community for whom it was built in 1675. The massive wooden barrel-vaulted ceiling is lit by more than 1,000 candles *(see p78)*.

4 Jodenbuurt
When the Jews arrived in Amsterdam in the late 16th century, they moved into a lacklustre area to the east of Oude Zijde, around present-day Waterlooplein. Although several synagogues, diamond factories and street markets have survived, the heart of the Jodenbuurt was decimated by post-war redevelopment and the building of the Metro. ✪ *Map Q5*

5 De Dokwerker
Mari Andriessen's evocative bronze statue (1952) is a memorial to the dockers' and transport workers' strike of February 1941 over the arrest of 450 Jews for the killing of a Nazi sympathizer. The event is commemorated every 25 February. ✪ *Jonas Daniel Meijerplein • Map Q5*

De Dokwerker

6 Hollandse Schouwburg
Jewish families were rounded up at this operetta theatre before being transported to the death camps. A moving memorial and a small exhibition of memorabilia keep their memory alive *(see p124)*.

Hollandse Schouwburg

Interior of the Tuschinski Theater

7 Tuschinski Theater

This extraordinary 1921 theatre was the creation of its obsessive owner, Abraham Tuschinski, a Jewish emigré who died at Auschwitz. The sumptuous interior crosses Art Deco with the Orient *(see p108)*.

8 Ravensbrück Memorial

Dedicated to the women of Ravensbrück, one of the most disturbing of the city's Holocaust memorials (1975) incorporates a sinister soundtrack and eerily flashing lights. ◈ *Museumplein* Map C6

9 Verzetsmuseum Amsterdam

The Resistance Museum's brilliant displays give a vivid sense of life in an occupied country, as well as an insight into the ingenious activities of the Dutch Resistance. Exhibits include photographs, heart-rending letters thrown from deportation trains, film clips and room sets *(see p124)*.

10 Nooit Meer

In stark contrast to its peaceful surroundings, Jan Wolkers' Auschwitz memorial *Never More* features a slab of shattered glass. The fragments reflect a distorted view of the heavens, mirroring the damage done to humanity by the Holocaust. ◈ *Wertheim Park* • Map R5

Top 10 Jewish Historical Events

1 1592 onwards
Sephardic Jews from Portugal and Spain, fleeing the Inquisition, settle in Amsterdam, attracted by the city's religious tolerance.

2 1630s
Ashkenazi Jews start to arrive from eastern Europe (mainly Poland and Germany).

3 1796
Jews are given equal civil rights during Napoleon's Batavian Republic.

4 1860
Drawn to Amsterdam by its new industries and housing, Jews emigrate from Antwerp.

5 1932–7
These years see the rise of the Dutch Nazi Party under Anton Mussert; they also see waves of Jewish immigration from Hitler's Germany.

6 1941
In February, nine months into the German Occupation, the dockworkers strike in protest at the arrest and round-up of 450 Jews.

7 1942
The deportation of the Jews to Nazi death camps begins. Many Jews, including Anne Frank's family, go into hiding. Of the 80,000 living in pre-war Amsterdam, only 5,000 will survive the war.

8 1945
Amsterdam is liberated by Canadian troops on 5 May.

9 1947
Anne Frank's diary is published *(see pp32–3)*.

10 1975
Violent protests break out against the destruction of the Jodenbuurt – the old Jewish Quarter – in the Nieuwmarkt.

Left **Spanjer & Van Twist** Right **Twee Zwaantjes**

🔟 Cafés

1 De Jaren
Wood, air, glass and light seem the building elements of this spacious, multi-levelled grand café. Page through international newspapers at the reading table, pile up your plate at the salad bar, or sun yourself beside the canal on one of the best terraces in town. ◈ *Nieuwe Doelenstraat 20 • Map N5*

Café de Jaren

2 De Kroon
Waiters in long white aprons glide beneath crystal chandeliers at the grandest of grand cafés, in the heart of Amsterdam's night-life district. The glassed-in balcony is a great late breakfast spot, there's a tango salon on Monday nights, and things hot up on Saturdays with a live DJ. ◈ *Rembrandtplein 17 • Map P6*

3 Engelbewaarder
The man at the next table may be writing a novel; the couple across the way arguing politics. An interesting, literary clientele gives an edge to this classic "brown café". There migh even be a jazz band playing, and some locals swear that the French-fries you can have with your beer are the best in town. ◈ *Kloveniersburgwal 59 • Map P4*

4 Hoppe
The dark wooden interior and tang of cigar smoke in the air are the very essence of the classic "brown café". Pink-faced old men enjoying one too many *jenevers*, smart young professionals on the way home from work, friends meeting up for beer and a gossip, populate this cheery Amsterdam institution. ◈ *Spui 18 • Map M5*

5 Het Blauwe Theehuis
"The Blue Teahouse" in the middle of the Vondelpark is a 1930s architectural treasure, a trendy night spot and a great terrace café all in one. Snack on well-filled sandwiches under the trees, dance the night away to DJs upstairs, or just stop by for coffee on your walk through the park. ◈ *Vondelpark 5 • Map B6*

6 Land van Walem
Sip a champagne cocktail on the canal-side terrace, or show of your latest designer wear to the fashionable crowd inside one of Amsterdam's most popular cafés Piles of magazines and intriguing artworks help while away the time. ◈ *Keizersgracht 449 • Map L6*

De Reiger

7 De Reiger is the king of the *eetcafés*. Join the contented local clientele eating good food, knocking back the wine and just chatting. ❧ *Nieuwe Leliestraat 34 • Map K2*

Spanjer & Van Twist

8 At this popular spot on one of the prettiest canals in town you'll find pleasant staff, a friendly, down-to-earth atmosphere, good sandwiches and salads, and a fine waterside terrace. ❧ *Leliegracht 60 • Map L2*

Eerste Klas

9 A station café? If that gives you the horrors, think again. A minute or two in this stunningly decorated, classy 19th-century former first-class waiting room, and you're transported back in time. Station bustle becomes part of the atmosphere – though when you're back on the platform, it comes as a shock to find there are no steam trains. ❧ *Platform 2b, Amsterdam Centraal Station, Stationsplein • Map P1*

Twee Zwaantjes

10 Join in a jolly sing-along (the sort of happy, beery songs you feel you know the words to even if they're in a foreign language), and have a drink with the real, pre-gentrification Jordanese. ❧ *Prinsengracht 114 • Map L2*

Eerste Klas, Centraal Station

Top 10 Types of Café

Bruin Café

1 Snug, smoky and old-fashioned, these brown cafés are places for beer and gossip.

Grand Café

2 Always grand in size, sometimes these cafés are grand in style too.

Eetcafé

3 *Eetcafé* means, unsurprisingly, Eat Café, and eat is exactly what you do in one. Good cooking at a little below restaurant prices.

Hip Hangouts

4 Some cafés flash their designer credentials – and attract a suitably hip and trendy crowd.

Music Cafés

5 Live music or top DJs make a good start to an evening of clubbing *(see pp54–5)*.

Games Cafés

6 Devotees of billiards, chess, darts or board games will find entire cafés given over to single pursuits.

Coffee & Cake

7 Sometimes there's no alcohol at all, just tea, coffee and more calories than you'd care to mention.

Nachtcafés

8 When all else is closed, these night cafés open their doors through the wee hours, though tread carefully – some may be a little seedy.

Gay Cafés

9 From the stylish to the sweaty, Amsterdam's famous gay cafés cater to all tastes.

"Coffeeshops"

10 Here, intoxicants take a different form, and smoking rather than drinking is the predominant activity.

For more cafés **See pp80, 81, 86, 87, 94, 97, 105, 113, 118, 119**

Left **Moko** Right **Getto**

Bars

1 Moko
Classic designer chairs are so liberally scattered about this hip lounge bar that you'd be excused for thinking you had wandered into a design museum. To reassure yourself that you haven't, order up one of the home-flavoured fruit vodkas, enjoy a meal, or repair to the large, shady terrace beside the canal, where you can escape the world of fashion altogether. 🌐 *Amstelveld 12 • Map E5*

2 Noa
IT wizards, followers of fashion, advertising executives and other representatives of hip, young Amsterdam crowd in to the place that set the trend for the new lounge bar scene. Rub shoulders with all of the above as you knock back the drinks or slurp up Japanese noodle soup before heading off to party the night away somwhere else. 🌐 *Leidsegracht 84 • Map K6*

3 Seymour Likely Lounge
Designed by artists, run by artists and populated by artists (as well as starry-eyed hopefuls), this has long been a favourite late-night, pre-party hangout. The music is loud and good, and they love you if you look right. 🌐 *Nieuwezijds Voorburgwal 250 • Map M3*

4 Winston International
Once, the Winston was hip though seedy, but a major refit in recent years has transformed it into one of the hottest places in town – a vortex for artists and musicians. A young, creative crowd comes here for the good DJs, live music and generally go-getting atmosphere. Spot the next generation of music stars, or just kick back and have a good time *(see p55)*.

5 De Duivel
Tiny, packed to the gills and very loud, "The Devil" attracts a young crowd from all over the world. Once upon a time the draw was hip-hop – and the chance of spotting a famous rap artiste at the bar. Now, times have moved on, the pace has changed, and the music is more likely to be on a classic funk tip. Get on down and shake your booty. 🌐 *Reguliersdwarsstraat 87 • Map N6*

Noa

For more bars See pp80, 86, 87, 94, 97, 102, 110, 118

Wijnand Fockink

6 Wijnand Fockink
Proeflokalen, the "tasting houses" of local distilleries, were once places to knock back a quick *jenever* (Dutch gin) before re-emerging into the winter's air. Crooked and cosy, with wooden barrels lining the walls, this one dates back nearly 300 years. Drop in for a quick one. ◉ *Pijlsteeg 31 • Map N3*

7 Admiraal
Join knowledgeable Amsterdammers and curious visitors to try Dutch gin or gloriously sticky liqueurs at this *proeflokaal*-cum-restaurant. Charm a local by asking for a translation of some of the odder liqueur names (most are unprintable). ◉ *Herengracht 319 • Map L4 • 020 625 4334 • €€€*

8 Getto
A haven of light and charm on the edge of Red Light District sleaze. Great cocktails, big smiles and a mixed, attitude-free clientele are all part of the magic formula. DJs, bingo evenings and other activities liven up the week – and there's a good restaurant too. ◉ *Warmoesstraat 51b • Map P2 • 020 421 5151 • €€*

9 Freddy's Bar
Named after the late Freddy Heineken (he of beer fame), who was a frequent guest, this quiet city-centre classic, complete with piano music, leather upholstery, soft lighting and discreetly friendly barman, is ideal for a classy pre-dinner drink. Dress up, act suave, and bring someone you want to impress. ◉ *Hotel De l'Europe, Nieuwe Doelenstraat • Map N5*

10 De Koe
Downstairs, people are tucking in to good, basic food; upstairs, they're shoulder to shoulder around the bar. Order a beer and you're instantly part of a no-nonsense neighbourhood bar atmosphere, with just a touch of merry mayhem, and everyone aiming headlong at a good night out. ◉ *Marnixstraat 381 • Map K6*

Left **Winston International** Right **Paradiso**

TOP 10 Clubs

1 Arena Hotel
Dating from 1890, this cool three-star hotel on the east side of town was originally a Roman Catholic orphanage, and later an asylum. On Fridays and Saturdays the madness continues, when some of Amsterdam's top DJs spin at Tonight, the hotel's adjacent two-floor "church-club". A bit of a trek if you're staying centrally, but worth the effort. ✆ 's Gravesandestraat 51 • Map G5 • 020 850 2400

2 Café West Pacific
DJs mix eclectic tunes in the quirky industrial setting of this unfailingly fabulous café-restaurant, part of the former Westergasfabriek gas factory complex. At weekends, the back bar (where the factory workers would scrub up) opens, and it gets very busy – so arrive early. ✆ Haarlemmerweg 8-10 • Map C1 • 020 488 7778

3 Mazzo
Whether your taste is fat beats, drum'n'bass, hip hop,

Café West Pacific

techno or electronic music, a variety of nights from Wednesday through Sunday ensure that this relaxed and friendly club caters to just about all tastes. If it doesn't cater to yours, pop across the road to More (see below). ✆ Rozengracht 114 • Map K3 • 020 626 7500

4 Melkweg
As well as regular parties that take place throughout the various rooms of this multi-media venue, DJs play before and after the live bands that appear on both stages. Most Saturdays there is a late-night dance party. ✆ Lijnbaansgracht 234a • Map K6 • 020 531 8181

5 More
Less definitely is more at this hip, minimalist hangout, owned by the proprietors of the Supperclub (see p86) and Nomads, the equally decadent, Arabian-style restaurant located upstairs (see p103). Amsterdam's beautiful people descend here at weekends – but only when they feel like it. ✆ Rozengracht 133 • Map J3 • 020 528 7459

6 NL-Lounge
A free-entry lounge club with a plush, carpeted interior – complete with armchairs. It's open daily, and delightfully decadent, although the drinks are a little on the pricey side. ✆ Nieuwezijds Voorburgwal 169 • Map M3 • 020 622 7510

Paradiso
Formerly a church, now predominantly a live music venue, DJs join here after the bands have been on with an emphasis Alternative music. The programming for parties can be erratic anything from Moroccan dance nights to cinema-club evenings. ◉ Weteringschans 6-8 • Map D5 • 020 626 4521

Panama
Monied 30-somethings with penchant for champagne make the trek to this lavish, vaudeville theatre-style club with attached bar and restaurant on the east side of town. Entry is expensive; the drinks aren't cheap either. ◉ Oostelijke Handelskade 4 • Map G2 • 020 311 8686 • €€€€

Vakzuid
This stylish and spacious bar-club-restaurant is unusually located within the grandstand of the stadium built for the 1928 Olympic Games, hosted by

Vakzuid

Amsterdam. Relax in lounge heaven as you look out onto the track. In good weather, the outdoor benches are unbeatable. ◉ Olympisch Stadion 35 • 020 570 8400 • €€€€

Winston International
Eclectic and inspired programming give this small, rococo-style venue an edge on the city's other clubs. Easy-tuners with a taste for the unusual head here for Sunday's Vegas nights. An additional plus: it boasts the smallest art gallery in Amsterdam – in its toilets. ◉ Warmoesstraat 129 • Map N3 • 020 623 1380

Left **Boom Chicago** Right **KIT Tropentheater**

Performing Arts Venues

1 De Balie
Politicians, artists, writers and film directors all rub shoulders at this highbrow cultural-political centre offering regular independent film screenings, lectures, debates, multi-media performances and exhibitions. There's also a spacious café, a restaurant (the latter only open in the evenings), and enough reading material to keep even the most demanding bookworm happy. ◎ *Kleine Gartmanplantsoen 10 • Map C5 • 020 553 5100*

2 Boom Chicago
On a daily basis, this US comedy crew puts on satirical shows whose targets are anything from Dutch "quirks" to topical news issues. Big on laughs and big on beer. The latter, served in huge pitchers, is a welcome respite from the tiny frothy-headed *pilsjes*. Star-watchers note: Burt Reynolds once popped in. ◎ *Leidseplein Theater, Leidseplein 12 • Map K6 • 020 423 0101*

3 Cristofori Salon
Classy classical recitals are held within this private, plushly restored concert hall on the upper floors of these former 17th-century coffee and tobacco warehouses. Named after the inventor of the piano, Italian Bartolommeo Cristofori, the repertoire regular extends to tango and jazz. ◎ *Prinsengracht 581–583 • Map K4 • 020 626 8485*

4 Carré
Originally built as a circus theatre in 1894, circus troupes still appear at this impressive landmark on the banks of the Amstel – along with anything from opera to ballet, magicians to music. Nothing beats sipping champagne on the balcony overlooking the river on a warm evening. ◎ *Amstel 115–125 • Map F5 0900 25 25 255*

5 Concertgebouw
The *crème de la crème* of international musicians and conductors appear at this palati cwlassical music venue – one o the world's most prestigious. Audrey Hepburn had a season ticket when she lived here after World War II, and it's not hard t understand why. Don't miss the free lunchtime concerts on Wednesdays *(see p115)*.

Concertgebouw

elix Meritis

9 Het Muziektheater

The Dutch royals regularly pop in to catch shows at this comfortable – and once controversial – modern theatre, which is home to the Netherlands Opera and Ballet companies *(see p78)*. Tickets for shows – particularly opera – can sell out months in advance, so it's advisable to book before you travel if you want to go. Inspired programming gives contemporary culture vultures an occasional look-in – Icelandic songstress Björk even played here once. ◎ *Amstel 3 • Map E4 • 020 625 5455*

6 Felix Meritis

In 1777, the Felix Meritis Society was founded to promote the arts and sciences. Ten years later, its wealthy members had this canal house specially built. To this day it stages international dance performances, theatre, lectures and electronic media events *(see p100)*.

7 Heineken Music Hall

Amsterdam's second biggest live music venue (the ArenA next door, home to Ajax football team, is the biggest). Some distance from the centre, but worth it to catch the likes of Garbage or The Chemical Brothers. ◎ *Heineken Music Hall, ArenA Boulevard 590 • 0900 300 1250*

8 KIT Tropentheater

Eclectic world music/theatre performances are appropriately staged in the theatre of the city's tropical museum *(see p127)*. Some world cinema is also to be had – though double-check the language the subtitles are in! ◎ *Mauritskade 63 / Linnaeusstraat 2 • Map G5 • 020 568 8500*

10 Stadsschouwburg

This Neo-Renaissance building – both of whose predecessors burned down – houses the city's municipal theatre. Local groups as well as visiting companies tread the boards here. It's also host to the annual Julidans (July Dance) Festival. Regular English-language performances take place in the upstairs Bovenzaal. ◎ *Leidseplein 26 • Map K6 • 020 624 2311*

Left *Patat* served with mayonnaise Right *Bitterballen*

Culinary Highlights

1 Maatjes Haring
Fresh raw herring, with chopped onion or gherkin, is sold as a snack from street stalls. Traditionally, you take your herring by the tail and toss it whole down your throat, with your head held back – but the faint-hearted may prefer them on a plate or in a roll. Best in May, when the *groene* (new season's) herrings appear.

2 Gerookte Paling
A delicious Dutch speciality, *paling* (smoked eel) comes from the IJsselmeer. Served with white toast and a squeeze of lemon, it makes a perfect starter.

3 Kaas
In the Netherlands, a staggering 14 kg (31 lb) of cheese per person is consumed each year. Gouda and Edam are the best known, but there are others, such as *Friese nagelkaas*, a clove cheese which became popular when spices were first imported in the 17th century.

4 Bitterballen
Served much like tapas to accompany drinks in a café or bar, these deep-fried meatballs have a crunchy exterior and a soft meat filling. They are served with mustard.

5 Hutspot
The Dutch love affair with potatoes manifests itself in a variety of hearty winter dishes. *Hutspot* (meaning hotchpotch) is a stew of braised beef and potatoes mashed with carrots, while *stamppot boerenkool* consists of mashed potato and cabbage flecked with chopped bacon and served with smoked sausage.

6 Erwtensoep
Like raw herring, this pea soup is another Dutch favourite that some foreigners find hard to love, with a consistency akin to wallpaper paste. Try it at Dorrius, which serves genuine Dutch food. ◉ *Nieuwezijds Voorburgwal 5* • Map N1

Erwtensoep

7 Rijsttafel
A delicious culinary after-echo of Holland's colonial past, Indonesian cuisine is usually eaten in the form of *rijsttafel* (rice table), a veritable feast consisting of as many as 25 little dishes of meat, fish, vegetables and sauces (some very hot), centred around a shared bowl of rice or noodles. Amsterdam has several good Indonesian restaurants, including Kantijl en de Tijger and Tujuh Maret *(see p61)*. ◉ *Kantijl en de Tijger: Spuistraat 291* • Map M4

8 Appelgebak
Puddings are very popular, particularly the classic apple pie, accompanied by a large dollop of whipped cream *(slagroom)*. By common consent, the best *appelgebak* in Amsterdam is served at Winkel. ◎ *Winkel: Noordermarkt 43 • Map D2*

Pannenkoeken

9 Pannenkoeken
Pancake houses offer an astonishing variety of fillings – try the Pancake Bakery *(see p97)* for an excellent selection. The traditional Dutch favourite is a large pancake topped with a thick syrup called *stroop*. If you have room for more, there are delicious, sugary *poffertjes*, the mini pancakes sold in summer from brightly painted stalls and from permanent stands at Dam Square and Leidesplein.

10 Patat
Served from street stalls in a handy paper cone, chips (french fries) are ubiquitous, and very good indeed. They are generally made from whole (not pulped) Dutch potatoes, and fried in good, clean fat. Served with a large dollop of mayonnaise, they are definitely not for the diet-conscious. For the very best, go to Vleminckx. ◎ *Vleminckx: Voetboogstraat 33 • Map M5*

Top 10 Drinks

1 Pils
The national drink of the Netherlands is beer. *Pils* – top brands Heineken and Grolsch – is the lager-like beer served (with froth) in bars. The Dutch generally drink it from small glasses, so it remains ice-cold to the last drop.

2 Witbier
Wheat-brewed white beer is pale and cloudy – often served with a slice of lemon.

3 Bockbier
A brown, sweet, winter beer served in round glasses.

4 Jonge Jenever
Dutch gin is flavoured with juniper and drunk neat – usually downed in a swift gulp from a small glass. *Jonge* (young) *jenever* is colourless and sharp.

5 Oude Jenever
Smoother, more complex, and slightly yellow in colour. Both types are referred to in bars as *borrel* (a tot).

6 Kopstoot
Aptly named, a *kopstoot* (head knock) is a *pils* swiftly followed by a *jenever* chaser.

7 Naveltje Bloot
Literally, Naked Tummy Button: a fruit liqueur traditionally taken when a mother-to-be shows off her bump to family and friends.

8 Oranje Bitter
An orange-flavoured liqueur knocked back on *Koninginnedag* (30 April).

9 Bakkie
A cup of strong black coffee, the way the Dutch prefer it.

10 Koffie Verkeerd
If you like your coffee milky, "wrong coffee" is what to ask for.

Left **Café Roux** Right **Mamouche**

🔟 Restaurants

1 Vossius
One of Holland's top chefs, Robert Kranenborg, surprises and delights the taste buds with such stunning creations as saddle of hare in a rich chestnut honey and cocoa sauce. Sit back in genteel grey-and-gold surroundings, select a heavenly wine, and permit yourself to be pampered. Expensive, but worth it. ⊗ *Hobbemastraat 2 • Map C5 • 020 577 4100 • €€€€€*

2 Van Vlaanderen
The décor may be plain, but the dishes are rich and elaborate at this gourmands' paradise, which for years was known only to insiders but recently acquired an international reputation when it picked up a long-deserved Michelin star. Expect to feast on goose-liver, suckling pig, pigeon breasts, sweetbreads and other delightfully wicked fare. ⊗ *Weteringschans 175 • Map E5 • 020 622 8292 • €€€€*

3 Lof
Tantalizing aromas from the open-plan kitchen, clanging pans and cheery banter fill the air at this friendly, bistro-style local favourite. Amsterdammers in the know come for scrumptious, imaginative cooking, taking pot-luck from a set menu that changes daily. ⊗ *Haarlemmerstraat • Map D2 • 020 620 2997 • €€€*

4 De Rode Leeuw
Join quietly munching old-timers, Dutch families and curious tourists in a cosily cluttered restaurant for a traditional Dutch meal. ⊗ *Damrak 93 • Map N3 • 020 555 0666 • €€€*

5 Café Roux
One of Amsterdam's smartest hotels is home to this classic, long-time favourite. It's realm of crisp linen, soft light and clinking glasses; the atmosphere is relaxed and the staff charming. Star chef Albert Roux inspires dishes with a fine French touch, such as brill with parsnip purée, salsify and thyme – and you can choose from a top-class wine list. (Note: Albert Roux is not the resident chef here, only a behind-the-scenes consultant.) ⊗ *The Grand Hotel, Oudezijds Voorburgwal • Map N4 • 020 555 3560 • €€€*

Lof

For more restaurants **See pp80, 81, 86, 94, 95, 102, 103, 110, 111, 113, 118**

Indochine

L'Indochine
6 Owner Kiet Anh Le flies in fresh ingredients for delicate Vietnamese dishes and spicier Thai cuisine. L'Indochine is not just an excellent Southeast Asian venue, but a superb restaurant in any category. Cream-and-white decor and a placid, watchful Buddha make for a calming atmosphere. Not to be missed. ◎ *Beulingstraat 9 • Map L5 • 020 627 9755 • €€€*

Tujuh Maret
7 Treating yourself to an Indonesian *rijsttafel* ('rice table') is an absolute must in Amsterdam – and this one is outstanding. Enjoy a feast of 18 deliciously spicy dishes, from mild to explosively chilli-filled, flavoured with coconut and ginger, peanuts and lemongrass, all served with mounds of rice. ◎ *Utrechtsestraat 73 • Map E5 • 020 427 9865 • €€*

Mamouche
8 Join a super-fashionable crowd in super-chic surroundings to experience the very best of Moroccan cuisine. Familiar dishes like lamb tagine and couscous share the menu with the chef's more elaborate creations, such as stewed rabbit and sesame with baked apricots and cinnamon seeds. ◎ *Quellijnstraat 104 • Map D6 • 020 673 7361 • €€€*

De Bolhoed
9 "Eclectic" hardly seems an adequate word for an interior that combines Dutch granny's knick-knacks with Thai statues and Australian aboriginal art, all against the background of a zany colour scheme, but this is the best vegetarian restaurant in town. Tuck in to big helpings with organic ingredients and a Mexican touch. ◎ *Prinsengracht 60 • Map L1 • 020 626 1803 • €*

Le Pêcheur
10 Crystal chandeliers, an elegant courtyard garden and genteel staff contribute to an atmosphere of timeless chic at this top, centrally located fish restaurant. Slip your lips around succulent oysters, revel in a classic *bouillabaisse* or go for something more adventurous, like roast monkfish with wild mushroom pasta, or flappingly fresh fish with an explosion of Thai spices. ◎ *Reguliersdwarsstraat 32 • Map M6 • 020 624 3121 • €€€€*

For a guide to restaurant prices **See p81**

Left **Bloemenmarkt** Right **Looiersmarkt**

🔟 Shops and Markets

1 Albert Cuypmarkt
Amsterdam's largest general market runs all the way down this long street in the Pijp area, touting everything from fresh fish to footwear. Come here for fabrics, but don't come here for clothes *(see p108)*.

Albert Cuypmarkt

2 Albert Heijn
Albert Heijn is a rather upmarket supermarket chain – there's at least one in each area of town. A little pricey, but the selection is wide, the aisles are wide, and they're wide awake: unusually, several centrally located branches stay open until 10pm. ◎ *Various branches*

3 De Bijenkorf
Named "The Beehive" (which just about sums it up if you're here at the weekend), Amsterdam's prestigious department store caters for everyone from children to clubbers. Often described as the Dutch Harrods, prices ensure

that it's only the well-honied that tend to part with their cash here ◎ *Dam 1 • Map N3*

4 Bloemenmarkt
Amsterdam's famous floating flower market – the stalls still float, but now they are permanent *(see p108)*.

5 Blokker
This cheap and cheerful chainstore purveying unintentionally kitsch interior supplies – be that a coffee cup or a toilet brush – has become something of an institution in the Netherlands. One regular customer even requested that her ashes should be scattered in one. ◎ *Various branches*

6 Boerenmarkt
Amsterdam's organic Saturday "farmer's market" is a treat rather than a routine shopping trip. Cruise the stalls to the accompaniment of some fine busking and sample free goats' cheese and other goodies – plus freshly-baked bread, flowers and a fabulous fungi selection. ◎ *Noordermarkt • Map D2*

7 Looiersmarkt
Burrow away to your heart's content in this highly browsable and perpetually intriguing indoor warren of antiques and collectibles. When you've dug out some bargains, there's also a café where you can put your weary feet up *(see p100)*.

Magna Plaza
8 Built between 1895 and 1899, this magnificent building – once derisively dubbed "post-office Gothic" by its critics – was designed by Cornelis Hendrik Peters (1874–1932) to house Amsterdam's head post office. Now a shopping mall, around 40 diverse stores are located over its three floors (the basement is currently not in use). There are two cafés. ⊗ *Nieuwezijds Voorburgwal 182 • Map M3*

Noordermarkt
9 There has been a market on this site since 1627 – a fact you can contemplate as you fight over the bargains with die-hard grubbers who arrive here after a night out, or with the locals who come for a civilized Monday morning rummage. Unbeatable for second-hand clothes and accessories *(see p92)*.

Waterlooplein
10 Whether your taste is exotic crafts and jewellery or vintage clothes, you can find them from Monday to Saturday at the city's best flea market – although it's a jumble at the best of times. When you can take no more, escape to the adjacent indoor markets. ⊗ *Map Q5*

Magna Plaza

Top 10 Souvenirs

Beer
1 There's more to Dutch beer than Heineken. The Dutch make a fabulous variety of beers, and you will find many of them at De Bierkoning *(see p87)*.

Bulbs
2 Check your country's import regulations before packing this fabulous floral souvenir into your luggage.

Cannabis
3 Don't even think about it.

Cheese
4 If you don't have time to make it to an out-of-town cheese market, visit De Kaaskamer *(see p104)* for a mouth-watering selection that's guaranteed to impress more than Edam or Gouda.

Clogs
5 The quintessential Dutch footwear; be in fashion, and be heard.

Condoms
6 Novelty condoms galore, and in a variety of flavours; the city's infamous Condomerie will oblige *(see p81)*.

Delftware
7 If you don't manage to snag one of the dishy Dutch, at least you can take home a Dutch dish.

Diamonds
8 Definitely a girl's best friend, but possibly the worst nightmare of the poor guy who has to fork out for them.

Jenever
9 "The father of gin" – the real thing, in a variety of flavours and bottle types.

T-shirts/Postcards
10 No shortage of T-shirts and postcards portraying anything from the utterly sublime to the absolutely ridiculous.

For more shops See pp81, 87, 104, 105, 112, 113, 119

Left **The Jordaan from the tower of the Westerkerk** Right **Leidseplein by night**

🔟 Walks and Cycle Rides

1 Jordaan
Start at Westerkerk *(see p91)*, perhaps climbing its tower for a bird's-eye view of the area. Work your way north to picturesque Brouwersgracht *(see p92)*.

2 Shopping Walk
Beginning at Noordermarkt *(see pp63, 92)*, take Prinsengracht to the Negen Straatjes *(see p100)* with its quirky shops. Have a look at De Looier antiques market in Elandsgracht *(see p62)* before heading down Lijnbaansgracht to Leidseplein. Turn up Leidsestraat and make for Metz & Co, with its top-floor café *(see p99)* – then on to Bloemenmarkt *(see pp63, 108)*, ending at De Bijenkorf on Damrak *(see p62)*.

3 Nightlife Walk
Start at the entertainment hub, Leidseplein *(see p101)*, before moving to the bright lights around Rembrandtplein *(see p107)*. Wind down at the junction of Reguliersgracht with

The Oude Schans

Herengracht, where you can see no less than 15 romantically lit bridges. Continue to Amstelkerk finishing in Utrechtsestraat, with its many appealing cafés and restaurants *(see p61, 110, 111)*.

4 Around Oude Schans
From Centraal Station, discover a quiet part of the old city by taking Binnenkant, lined with fine houses, and then, passing Montelbaanstoren, walking along Oude Schans to reach the Rembrandthuis *(see p77)*. Pause at De Sluyswacht, the crooked café on the bridge *(see p80)*, before exploring the old Jewish quarter, Jodenbuurt *(see p48)*, or continuing to Nieuwmarkt *(see p77)*.

5 Herengracht
Shortest and most fascinating of the Grachtengordel *(see pp8-11)*, the Herengracht is lined with beautiful buildings, such as the Bartolotti House *(see p91)*, the Bijbels Museum *(see p99)* and the mansions of the Golden Bend *(see p8)*.

6 To Ouderkerk aan de Amstel
For a tranquil cycle ride, follow the Amstel from the city centre (start near Blauwbrug) to Ouderkerk aan de Amstel *(see p128)*. The route passes Amstelpark and the De Rieker windmill *(see p127)* before entering attractive countryside. About 20 km (12 miles) round trip.

7 Plantage

With its distinguished villas, tree-lined streets, parks and gardens, Plantage (see pp122-5) is a calm district to explore by bike (with the exception of busy Plantage Middenlaan).

8 Prinsengracht

At 3 km (2 miles), the outermost canal of the Grachten-gordel (see p8) is quite tiring on foot, but makes a very pleasant, fairly car-free cycle ride, with plenty of cafés at which to rest along the way.

9 Western Islands

Perhaps the most peaceful part of Amsterdam in which to walk or cycle lies to the north-west of Centraal Station. The islands of Prinseneiland, Bickerseiland and Realeneiland, together known as the Western Islands, have a remote, bracing quality, with well-worn boatyards and white drawbridges, as well as modern housing (see p93).

10 Amsterdamse Bos

This attractive wooded park south of the city is ideal for cyclists, thanks to 48 km (30 miles) of cycle path; those on foot have no less than 160 km (100 miles) of footpath to stroll along. Perfect for a family picnic outing (see p128).

Prinsengracht

Top 10 Tips for Cycling in Amsterdam

1 Stick to the Rules

Don't copy the locals, who frequently jump red lights and ride on sidewalks.

2 Stay in the Cycle Lanes

Amsterdam has an excellent integrated network of fietspaden (cycle lanes), with white lines, cycle signs and dedicated traffic lights.

3 Cross Tramlines with Care

If you have to, cross tramlines at an angle, to avoid your front wheel getting stuck.

4 Avoid Trams

They are bigger than you, and can't be steered; listen for their rattle and stay clear.

5 Watch for Pedestrians

It's usually tourists who mistakenly walk in cycle lanes; keep an eye out for parked cars, too.

6 Give Priority

Motorists and cyclists have priority when entering your road from the right.

7 Dismount at Busy Junctions

Unless you are really confident, it's better to negotiate these on foot.

8 Don't Cycle Two-Abreast

It's only allowed if you are not obstructing the traffic; otherwise, stay in single file.

9 Use Lights

By law, you must turn your lights on after dusk – you must also have reflector bands on both wheels.

10 Lock Your Bike

Bicycle theft is rife. Make sure that you always lock both front wheel and frame to an immovable object.

Left **De Star Hofje** Right **Egelantiersgracht**

Places for Peace and Quiet

1 De Star and Zon's Hofjes
These two charming courtyards, just a few paces from each other, offer the weary visitor a calm retreat from the crowds *(see p92)*.

2 Museum Van Loon
Behind Adriaan Dortsman's grand façade, the Van Loon family residence has a calm, welcoming feel. Lose yourself in the intimate, elegantly furnished rooms, or in the charming rose garden with its 18th-century coach house disguised as a Neo-Classical temple *(see pp30–31)*.

18th-century sledge, Museum Van Loon

3 Zandhoek
Only a few minutes away from the bustle of central Amsterdam, Zandhoek (on Realeneiland in the Western Islands) feels remote and slow-paced. Cobbles, white draw-bridges, 17th-century buildings

and splendid old barges moored along the harbour front make a picturesque sight *(see p93)*.

4 Binnenkant
Bordering Waalseilands-gracht, an attractive side-canal dotted with houseboats, Binnenkant is lined with fine old merchants' houses. A couple of well-placed benches at the junction with Kalkmarkt allow you to sit and contemplate a charming stretch of the Oude Schans, site of the city's first shipyards, and the fortified Montelbaanstoren towering above it *(see p79)*. ◈ Map Q3

5 Café de Sluyswacht
A few steps down from busy Jodenbreestraat brings you to the crooked Café de Sluyswacht *(see p80)* with its spacious terrace, where tables and chairs are set out at the merest hint of fine weather. A surprisingly tranquil spot, from here you enjoy a different perspective of the Oude Schans.

6 Grimburgwal
This peaceful corner of the Oude Zijde at the convergence of three canals was a popular spot for medieval convents: appropriately, one of the side streets is called Gebed Zonder End (Prayer Without End). If you need to rest, there are benches on Oudezijds Voorburgwal, just beyond the Huis op de Drie Grachten. ◈ Map N5

7 Hortus Botanicus

A wild and verdant place dotted with tropical palmhouses and welcome benches, the small botanical garden on the east side of the city dates back to 1682, when an apothecary's herb garden was established here (see p124).

8 Theatermuseum Garden

A café at the back of this museum in an elegant 1638 house by Philips Vingboons has tables and chairs that spill out into a glorious, mature garden – the perfect place to recharge your batteries (see p91).

9 Egelantiersgracht

The Westerkerk carillon might be the only sound to break the silence as you stroll along this pretty side-canal in the Jordaan bordered by artisans' dwellings. At Nos 107–14, St Andrieshofje, built in 1616, is one of the city's oldest and best reserved almshouses. A charming blue-and-white tiled passage leads from the street into the courtyard (see p92). Map J2

10 Overloop-plantsoen

This sleepy little park nestles at the junction of two canals, Nieuwe Keizersgracht and Plantage Muidergracht. ◈ Map R6

Theatermuseum garden

Top 10 Vantage Points

1 Westerkerk Tower
Climb Amsterdam's tallest tower to see the attractive jumble of the Jordaan below (see p91).

2 Zuiderkerk Tower
The top of the Zuiderkerk gives a vista of the former Jewish quarter (see p42).

3 Oude Kerk Tower
See the medieval city and the red-light district from this tower (see p29).

4 Metz & Co
The city's most impressive canal views are from the sixth-floor café and the cupola perched on top (see p99).

5 Madame Tussaud's Scenerama
The round window on the top floor offers a terrific view of Dam Square (see p35).

6 Amstelveld
From this peaceful square at the junction of Reguliersgracht and Prinsengracht, there are pretty stretches of the canal in both directions.

7 Magere Brug
Stand on this bridge at night for splendid views of the Amstel (see p11).

8 Reguliersgracht and Herengracht
Put Thorbeckeplein behind you and count 15 bridges from this junction – a spectacular sight after dark.

9 Bloemgracht
The best view of this lovely side-canal is from the junction with 1e Bloemdwars-straat (see p9).

10 NEMO
Climb the broad outside stairs to the roof for a striking view across the Oosterdok to the city (see p129).

Left **Artis Zoo** Right **NEMO**

Children's Attractions

1 East Indiaman Amsterdam
This splendid replica of a Dutch East India Company ship that sank on its maiden voyage in 1749 makes a fine sight in Oosterdok. Visit the captain in his luxurious cabin and the cook in his galley, and watch the sailors hoisting cargo and swabbing decks *(see p123)*.

East Indiaman Amsterdam

2 Canal Bikes
Explore the canals at your own pace. Adults may find these pedal boats energy-sapping, but children will love them. They seat either two or four people, and can be boarded at four different central locations *(see p135)*.

3 Tram Rides
Take the Circle Tram (No. 20) and see Amsterdam's main sights in one ride. Or go to Haarlemmermeer railway station and take a 20-minute ride in an old-fashioned tram with wooden seats, clanging bell and friendly conductor to Amsterdamse Bos, where you will find pancakes, peacocks, and plenty of leg-stretching space. ✪ *Electrische Museumtramlijn: Haarlemmermeerstation Amstelveenseweg 264 • 020 673 7538 • www.trammuseum.demon.nl • Trams depart Apr–Oct: 11am–5:05 pm Sun; Jul: 1:45–3:15pm Wed • Admission charge*

4 Puppet Shows
There has been a puppet theatre on Dam Square for over a hundred years. Puppet Theatre Pantijn performs every Wednesday afternoon in summer. If it's raining, go to their theatre in Sint Pieterspoortsteeg 33, where the show takes place at 2pm, 3.30pm and 4pm *(see p35)*. ✪ *Puppet Theatre Pantijn: 020 627 9188 • Free*

5 NEMO
It's worth going to Amsterdam's science and technology centre just for the building – dubbed "Titanic" by locals – and for the superb view from the roof. Inside, enquiring minds will be kept alert with scores of fun, thought-provoking demonstrations of the world around us *(see p129)*.

6 Artis Zoo
Children love this action-packed zoo, where they can pat the animals in the children's farm, brave the steamy reptile house, see the stars in the planetarium, and marvel at the fish in the vast aquarium *(see p123)*.

Vondelpark

7 This is the perfect place to go with kids on a summer day – has a paddling pool, playgrounds, puppet shows and facepainting (at the Melkhuis café), as well as free performances in the open-air theatre *(see p115)*.

Church Towers

8 The tallest, at 85 m (276 ft), is the tower of Westerkerk *(see p91)*, where the reward is not just a great view, but the city's heaviest bell and the gaily painted imperial crown of Maximilian of Austria, his gift to the city. The towers of Oude Kerk *(see p29)* and Zuiderkerk *(see p42)* can also be climbed.

Tropenmuseum

9 Stroll through a highly realistic North African street, Indian village or Arab market – all at the Tropenmuseum. There is also a "hands-on" Kindermuseum (Children's Museum), which is open to 6- to 12-year-olds by appointment (guided tours in Dutch only) *(see p127)*.

Madame Tussaud's Scenerama

10 If you want to take a trip back into the days of the Golden Age, experience a moon landing, or meet Michael Jackson and a host of other stars, then this waxworks is the place. There's a great view of Dam Square from the round window, too *(see p35)*.

Kindermuseum

Top 10 Sights and Sounds for Free

1 Civic Guards Gallery
Huge portraits of the Civic Guard at the Amsterdams Historisch Museum *(see p26)*.

2 Begijnhof
A haven of peace and tranquillity right in the centre of the city *(see p22–3)*. For more delightful *hofjes* in the Jordaan, see p92.

3 Hollandse Manege
Stylish 19th-century royal riding school *(see p117)*.

4 Rijksmuseum Garden
Architectural curiosities in a formal garden *(see p14)*.

5 Lunchtime Concerts
At the Concertgebouw every Wednesday at 12:30pm *(see p119)* and at the Boekmanzaal in the Stadhuis *(see p78)* every Tuesday at 12:30pm, October to June.

6 Ferry across the IJ
Join the locals on the five-minute ferry ride from Centraal Station *(see p84)* to North Amsterdam.

7 Bloemenmarkt
Locals and tourists alike love the Singel's colourful floating market *(see p108)*.

8 Seven European Houses
See Europe in a minute at Roemer Visscherstraat 20–30a – a row of houses in the style of seven countries *(see p148)*.

9 Barrel Organs
A joyful feature of Amsterdam's streets – there are eight of them in all.

10 Church Bells
The carillons of the Westertoren, Zuidertoren and Munttoren unleash their glorious peals from noon–1pm on Tuesdays, Thursdays and Fridays respectively.

Left **Queen's Day bric-a-brac sale** Right **Queen's Day revellers**

Festivals and Events

1 Nationaal Museumweekend

Most of Amsterdam's state-run museums participate in this scheme, run by SMJK (Stichting Museumjaarkaart), to offer free or reduced-price entry for one weekend. Details are published through the Tourist Board in mid-March. ◈ *mid-Apr*

2 Koninginnedag

On the Queen's birthday, the whole city becomes a gigantic street party. The locals sell bric-a-brac from stalls outside their houses, there's a fair in Dam Square, and people dressed in monarchist orange throng the streets. Music blares, fireworks fill the night sky, and the party goes on till dawn. ◈ *30 April*

3 Bevrijdingsdag

The day after *Herden-kingsdag* (Remembrance Day), Liberation Day celebrates the end of the Nazi occupation with impromptu speeches, concerts and open-air markets in the Vondelpark, Leidseplein, Museumplein and Rokin. ◈ *5 May*

4 Holland Festival

An exciting programme of theatre, music, opera, ballet and art staged at various venues in and beyond the city, the Holland Festival has earned itself a prestigious reputation, attracting top-flight performers from the Netherlands and abroad. ◈ *020 530 7110 • www.hollandfestival.nl • Jun*

5 Open Monumentendagen

An exciting opportunity to see what lies behind the gabled façades and medieval doorways of some of the city's most historic buildings, which are open to the public for free over this weekend. ◈ *020 422 2118 • www.openmonumentendagen • Second weekend in Sep*

6 Bloemen Corso

In a spectacular procession, floats proceed from Aarlsmeer, home of the flower industry *(see p72)*, to Dam Square, weighed down by countless varieties of flowers – but not tulips, which are out of season. Watch from Vijzelstraat rather than join the crush in the Dam. The illuminated floats make a magical return journey. ◈ *First Sat in Sep*

7 Grachtenfestival

National and international stars perform classical music concerts at 20 historic locations around the three canals of the

Bloemen Corso

Prinsengrachtconcert, Grachtenfestival

Grachtengordel *(see p11)*. The highlight is a free piano recital given on a barge on Prinsengracht opposite the Pulitzer Hotel. ◈ *020 421 4542 • www.grachtenfestival.nl • 2nd or 3rd Wed–Sun in Aug*

8 Jordaan Festival

This picturesque district *(see p92)* makes an ideal setting for a low-key early-autumn festival. The local talent comes out of the woodwork for contests on Elandsgracht, and there are concerts, street parties and fairs – like the one devoted to food in Noordermarkt. ◈ *020 626 5587 • www.jordaanfestival.nl • mid-Sep*

9 Sinterklaas' Parade

The Christmas festivities start here. St Nicholas – the Dutch Santa Claus – arrives near St Nicholaas Kerk by boat with his mischievous elves, *Zwarte Pieten* (Black Peters). Together, they distribute sweets and gifts to the children of Amsterdam. ◈ *Second or third Sat in Nov*

10 New Year's Eve

New Year's Eve starts slowly and explodes into life at midnight with firework displays (there's an organized one over the Amstel) and wild street-partying centred on Nieuwmarkt and Dam Square. As with all events of this sort, things can sometimes get out of hand. ◈ *31 Dec*

Top 10 Spectator Sports

1 Football
See Ajax at their remarkable 50,000-seater stadium. ◈ *Amsterdam ArenA, Bijlmer • Aug–Dec, Feb–May*

2 Cycling
The RAI Derny Race is Amsterdam's only criterium (road circuit). ◈ *Amsterdam RAI, Europaplein • mid-May*

3 Basketball
The top local team is Ricoh Astronauts . ◈ *Sporthallen Zuid • Sep–mid-May*

4 Korfbal
A cross between netball and basketball. Blauw Wit is the club to watch. ◈ *Sportpark Joos Banckersweg • Sep–Jun*

5 Hockey
Amsterdamsche Hockey & Bandy Club are the ones to watch. ◈ *Wagener Stadium, Amstelveen • Sep–May*

6 Ice Hockey
The city supports the popular Boretti Tigers. ◈ *Sporthal Jaap Edenhal, Radioweg 64 • Oct–late Mar*

7 American Football
If you can't get tickets to watch Ajax, the Amsterdam Admirals also play at the ArenA *(see above)*. ◈ *Mar–Jun*

8 Running
The Amsterdam Marathon began in 1976 and is now an annual event. ◈ *Amsterdam RAI, Europaplein • Late Sep*

9 Rowing
Popular among the numerous competitions is the Head of the Amstel River race. ◈ *Last week Mar*

10 Show-jumping
Jumping Amsterdam is a series of international indoor competitions. ◈ *Amsterdam RAI, Europaplein • Nov/Dec*

Left **Haarlem** Right **Hortus Botanicus, Leiden**

🔟 Excursions

1 Aalsmeer Bloemenveilingen

Witnessed from an elevated viewing gallery, the world's largest flower auction is an astonishing sight. With flowers, speed is of the essence, and the atmosphere is frenetic. Bidding is highly automated, using the "backwards" Dutch clock system: the clock starts at 100, then counts down until the first bidder to press his button stops the auction and wins.

2 Delft

Sleepy Delft was shaken by a gunpowder explosion in 1654, after which the town was rebuilt – as recorded in *A View of Delft* by Vermeer around 1660. Since then, little has changed. There are Delft tiles in the Museum Lambert van Meerten, and in the shops. In Het Prinsenhof you can see the bullet holes left by the murder of William of Orange; his mausoleum is in the Nieuwe Kerk.

3 The Hague

Political capital of the Netherlands, Den Haag (The Hague) is a stately city, with many public buildings and lovely parks. Centred round the Gothic Ridderzaal, places of interest include the parliament buildings, the International Court of Justice and the Mauritshuis, elegant home of the superlative Royal Picture Gallery. The seaside resort of Scheveningen is a short distance away.

4 Enkhuizen

The fortunes of this attractive former fishing port declined dramatically after the construction of the huge Afsluitdijk in 1932 created the freshwater IJsselmeer and cut it off from the North Sea. Today it is home to the wonderful Zuiderzee Museum, which includes a reconstruction of a typical fishing village with costumed "inhabitants" and craftsmen at work.

5 Haarlem

Centred around the Grote Markt, with its buzzing pavement cafés and lovely buildings, the historic centre of this lively, well-heeled city is a delight. Highlights include the Frans Hals Museum, the Grote Kerk with its magnificent decorated Müller organ, and the Art Deco train station. Also well worth a visit is the Teylers Museum, with its excellent collection of science, technology and art exhibits.

Lime kilns, **Zuiderzee Museum, Enkhuizen**

6 Keukenhof

Throughout spring, but climaxing in mid-April when the tulips flower, a drab coastal strip between Leiden and Haarlem bursts into colour. Among these commercial bulbfields is the wooded Keukenhof park, the showcase for Dutch bulbs, a dazzling and unforgettable sight between late March and late May.

7 Leiden

An easy-going university town, full of cycling students, Leiden offers plenty of canals, cafés and museums, as well as the lovely Hortus Botanicus.

8 Marken

Just 16 km (10 miles) from Amsterdam, this former island fishing community, now reached by a narrow causeway, makes a refreshing day trip. Its distinctive wooden houses are charming, and the inhabitants wear traditional costume in summer.

9 Paleis Het Loo

Built in 1686 by Stadholder William III as a hunting lodge, Het Loo, near Apeldoorn, was a royal summer residence until the

Wooden house, Marken

1960s. Behind a sober façade lies a sumptuous interior, with rooms decorated to reflect the different eras of occupation, from the 1680s to the 1930s. There are also superb formal gardens to enjoy.

10 Utrecht

Like Leiden, Utrecht is a university city with much to offer – notwithstanding the vast, unappealing Hoog Catherijne shopping complex. A major medieval religious centre, it still has many traces of its past, and a lovely historic town centre.

Visit the Frans Hals Museum website at www.franshalsmuseum.nl
Visit the Paleis Het Loo website at www.hetloo.nl

AROUND TOWN

AMSTERDAM'S TOP 10

Left **Stopera** Right **Museum Het Rembrandthuis**

Oude Zijde

THE STREETS OF THE OUDE ZIJDE (OLD SIDE) *are packed with historic and beautiful buildings, though many are buried in the seediest parts. As the name suggests, this is where Amsterdam has its roots; the city grew from a ribbon of land on the eastern bank of the Amstel between Damrak and Oudezijds Voorburgwal (which means "before the city wall"). Today, the Oude Zijde incorporates the medieval city, built around the Oude Kerk, and the area to the east, where development started in the 15th century and continued over the following two centuries to accommodate Jewish émigrés. An area of richness and contrasts, within its boundaries lie the Nieuwmarkt* (dominated by the Waag, a 15th-century city gate turned weigh-house), the university quarter, Chinatown, the Red Light district, and what remains of the old Jodenbuurt (see p48), where four former synagogues have been combined to form the superb Joods Historisch Museum.

Oude Kerk

Sights

1. Oude Kerk
2. Nieuwmarkt
3. Museum Het Rembrandthuis
4. Agnietenkapel
5. Red Light District
6. Stopera
7. Joods Historisch Museum
8. Portugees-Israëlitische Synagoge
9. Hash Marihuana Hemp Museum
10. Montelbaanstoren

The Waag, Nieuwmarkt

Oude Kerk

1 The oldest church in Amsterdam has been altered and extended over the years, producing a heavenly jumble of architectural styles from medieval to Renaissance *(see pp28–9)*.

Nieuwmarkt

2 This vast open square has been a marketplace since the 15th century, and is still the scene of a Sunday antiques market in summer. Alone in the middle stands the bulky Waag (1488), bristling with turrets. The eastern gate in the city's defences, it was originally called St Antoniespoort. In the 17th century it became a weigh-house and home to numerous guilds, including the surgeons'. It was here that Rembrandt painted his famous *Anatomy Lesson of Dr Tulp*, now in the Mauritshuis, The Hague. There were few problems acquiring bodies for dissection, since public executions took place in the Nieuwmarkt. ✪ *Map P3*

Museum Het Rembrandthuis

3 Major refurbishment has recreated the interior as it might have been in Rembrandt's time. Of special interest are pictures by his master, Pieter Lastman. One room contains exotic collectibles of the day – busts of Roman emperors, spears and shells – as well as Rembrandt's precious art books and an inventory of his effects *(see p15)*. ✪ *Jodenbreestraat 4 • Map Q5 • 020 520 0400 • www. rembrandthuis.nl • Open 10am–5pm Mon–Sat, 1–5pm Sun & public hols • Admission charge*

Agnietenkapel

4 In the Oude Zijde's tranquil southwestern corner, what was, until the Alteration *(see p21)*, the chapel of St Agnes' convent (1470), is now the museum of the University of Amsterdam. On the first floor, still in use, is the oldest lecture room in the country, with a splendid painted ceiling and portrait gallery of humanist scholars. ✪ *Oudezijds Voorburgwal 231 • Map N4 • 020 525 3339 • Open 9am–5pm Mon–Fri • Free*

Red Light District

5 The world's oldest profession aptly occupies Amsterdam's oldest quarter, de Walletjes ("the little walls"), bordered by Zeedijk, Kloveniersburgwal, Damstraat and Warmoesstraat. Today, the district is one of the city's greatest tourist attractions, with scantily clad prostitutes, pouting or indifferent, sitting in windows or lolling in doorways along Oudezijds Voorburgwal and the lanes off it. At night these lanes become the haunts of junkies and pickpockets, and are best avoided. ✪ *Map P2, P3*

Red Light District

6 Stopera

With the Dutch penchant for clever wordplay, the Stadhuis-Muziektheater is better known as "Stopera" because it combines the *stadhuis* (town hall) with the headquarters of the city opera and ballet companies. A brutal design in red brick, marble and glass, it was built in 1987 amid intense controversy, since scores of medieval houses, among Jodenbuurt's few remnants, had to be destroyed in the process. In the passage between Stopera's two buildings, a bronze button indicates the exact NAP (*Normaal Amsterdams Peil*) water level. ◎ *Waterlooplein 22 • Map Q5 • Stadhuis: 020 552 9111. Open 8.30am–3.30pm Mon–Fri, 5–7pm Thu • Muziektheater: 020 625 5455*

7 Joods Historisch Museum

Abel Cahen's prize-winning design for the Jewish Historical Museum (1987) is a perfect marriage of old and new: the four synagogues that house it, built by Ashkenazi Jews during the 17th and 18th centuries, are linked by glass-covered internal walkways. Highlights of the exhibition, which is concerned with all aspects of Jewish life,

Joods Historisch Museum

are the Holy Ark (1791), focus of the Nieuwe Synagoge, the illuminated Haggadah manuscript (1734), and Elias Bouman's airy 17th-century Grote Synagoge *(see pp48–9)*. ◎ *Jonas Daniel Meijerplein 2–4 • Map Q5 • 020 626 9945 • www.jhm.nl • Open 11am–5pm daily • Admission charge*

8 Portugees-Israëlitische Synagoge

The Sephardic Jews, who settled in Amsterdam from the late 16th century, celebrated their new lives in a tolerant society a century later by commissioning Elias Bouman to build this imposing synagogue. It follows a traditional design with the Hechal (Holy Ark), facing Jerusalem, opposite the tebah, from where the cantor leads the service. The men sit on wooden benches downstairs, the women in a gallery above *(see p48)*. ◎ *Mr Visserplein 3 • Map R5 • 020 624 5351 • Open 10am–4pm daily • Closed Sat & Jewish hols • Admission charge*

9 Hash Marijuana Hemp Museum

Seen through a cloud of incense, exhibits in this tiny but fascinating museum chart the history of hemp (marijuana) from its earliest use some 8,000 years ago to the 20th-century drug

---

Modern-day Tolerance

In line with Amsterdam's long tradition of tolerance, the authorities generally overlook the possession and consumption of small quantities of cannabis or marijuana, although they are illegal. Their sale and use at regulated coffee shops *(see p51)* is officially accepted, but hard drugs and advertising are not. In 1990, brothels and the display of girls in their windows were legalized, although street prostitution remains illegal.

ars. As *hennep*, it was used in Holland for making lace, linens, fishing nets and fabric for sails, and processed by special windmills called *hennepkloppers*. There are displays about smuggling, an array of hookahs and reefers, and a "grow room" where plants are cultivated. ◎ *Oudezijds Achterburgwal 148 • Map P3 • 20 623 5961 • Open 11am–10pm daily • Admission charge*

Montelbaanstoren

A fortified tower, the Montelbaanstoren was built in 1512 on the eastern edge of Amsterdam, just outside the city wall. Its original purpose was to defend the Dutch fleet; now, more prosaically, it houses the Amsterdam water authority. The open-work steeple was added by the ubiquitous Hendrick de Keyser in 1606, when the city fathers felt that they could at last afford the icing on the cake. It overlooks the lovely Oude Schans (see p64), a canal that also dates from the early 16th century, dug to improve access for ships. ◎ *Oude Schans 2 • Map R3*

Montelbaanstoren

A Day in the Oude Zijde

Morning

As the Oude Kerk does not open until 11am, start your day with a tour of the **Museum Amstelkring** (see pp20–1). Although in the Nieuwe Zijde, it is only a few steps from the **Oude Kerk** (see pp28–9), which you can visit afterwards. Then walk to **Nieuwmarkt** (see p77) for a break at In de Waag (Nieuwmarkt 4), where you can sit outside in summer and watch the bustle of the square.

Afterwards, make your way to Oudezijds Achterburgwal for the **Hash Marijuana Hemp Museum**. Then follow the main drag of the **Red Light district** (see p77), Oudezijds Voorburgwal, as far as Café Roux (see p60) for lunch.

Afternoon

Walk down to peaceful Grimburgwal and the House on the Three Canals. **Agnietenkapel** is a few doors away. From here, head east to Oudezijds Achterburgwal and cut through Oudemanhuispoort (stone spectacles mark the entrance), browsing through the second-hand bookstalls as you go. Continue to Jodenbreestraat and the **Museum Het Rembrandthuis** (see p77). After your tour – if it is a Monday, Wednesday or Friday – pop into Pintohuis (see p44) for a glimpse of the painted ceiling. Revive yourself in Café de Sluyswacht (see p80). From here there is a lovely canalside walk, past the **Montelbaanstoren**. Turn left and stroll along Binnenkant before heading back to your hotel.

Left **Wijnand Fockinck** Right **In 't Aepjen**

Restaurants, Cafés and Bars

1 Bird
Those in the know flock here for the tastiest Thai in town. Eat in their spacious restaurant or duck out to their snackbar opposite for a more informal, utterly authentic experience. ◎ *Zeedijk 72 •Map P2 • 020 620 1442 • €€*

2 Getto
Kitsch and quirky, this friendly gay bar-restaurant is one of the best in town. Unbeatable cocktails, delicious home-cooked food, tarot readings (Sundays), occasional live DJ *(see p53)*.

3 In 't Aepjen
This unusual bar is located in one of the oldest wooden houses in the city (1551). Sailors would pay for their stay in monkeys – hence the primate theme in evidence throughout *(see p44)*.

4 Maximiliaan
In 1544, the nuns at this cloister started making beer, a tradition that was revitalized a few years ago – and there's a fine restaurant. ◎ *Kloveniersburgwal 6-8 • Map P4 • 020 626 6280*

5 De Sluyswacht
Rembrandt sketched this leaning former lock-keeper's house. There's a peaceful canalside terrace at the back. ◎ *Jodenbreestraat 1 • Map Q4*

6 Tis Fris
The best breakfasts in the area are served in this bright an airy café. Perfect before tackling the nearby Waterlooplein marke or for a caffeine break mid-browse. ◎ *St Antoniesbreestraat 142 Map P4*

7 VOC Café
Housed in the city's oldest defence tower, the Schreierstoren *(see p10)*, this spacious traditional-style bar ha a "reading room" out back and two terraces overlooking the water. ◎ *Prins Hendrikkade 94 • Map C*

8 Wijnand Fockink
Barely looking a day older than its 1679 origins, this is the best *proeflokaal* (tasting house) in town. The hidden garden out back is one of the city's best kept secrets *(see p52)*.

9 Lime
One of the hippest and friendliest bars in the area, yet decidedly unpretentious. ◎ *Zeed 104 • Map P3*

10 Blauw aan de Wal
An absolute treasu in the heart of the Red Light District, this Mediterranean restaurant should b savoured for hours. ◎ *Oudezijds Achter-burgwal 99 • Map P4 • 020 330 225 • €€€€*

Price Categories

For a three course meal for one with half a bottle of wine (or equivalent meal), taxes and extra charges.

€	under €20
€€	€20–€30
€€€	€30–€45
€€€€	€45–€60
€€€€€	over €60

atei

10 Best of the Rest

1 Condomerie
A huge, hilarious range of (mostly) novelty condoms guaranteed to spice up the most jaded of love lives. ◉ Warmoesstraat 141 • Map N3

2 Fo Kuang Shan Temple
This nun-run Chinese Buddhist temple takes pride of place on this otherwise junkie-riddled street. Take a respectful peek one afternoon (you can keep your shoes on), or dine at their adjacent vegetarian restaurant. ◉ Zeedijk 118 • Map P3 • €

3 Himalaya
A veggie café at the back of this new age bookstore overlooking the water is a fantastic find in this hectically touristy area. Chill out, Zen-style. ◉ Warmoesstraat 56 • Map P2

4 Jacob Hooy & Co
Established in 1743, this chemist's store is simply the best place in town to pick up herbs, homeopathic remedies, tea and essential oils. ◉ Kloveniersburgwal 12 • Map P3

5 Joe's Vliegerwinkel
Colourful kites, quirky knick-knacks and kitsch bits for that perfect present to suit all ages. ◉ Nieuwe Hoogstraat 19 • Map P4

6 Latei
A delightful café cum bric-a-brac store specializing in olive oil and Finnish wallpaper. Ideal for a light sandwich, fresh juice and decent-sized coffees. Everything is for sale. ◉ Zeedijk 143 • Map P3

7 RMF Streetwear International
Amsterdam's first hip hop shop has a fantastic range of US streetwear, including Ecko, Maurice Malone and Southpole. ◉ Oudezijds Voorburgwal 189 • Map P3

8 T-Boat
Amsterdam's only coffee-shop on a boat. With its lockside location on a wide canal near the Waterlooplein, the deck is the perfect spot for a refreshing drink or a quiet puff as the sun sets. ◉ By Oudeschans 143 • Map Q4

9 Tibet
Quite a find in the seedy surrounds of the Red Light District, this restaurant serves food until 1am. A mind-blowing menu that won't break the bank. ◉ Lange Niezel 24 • Map P2 • 020 624 1137 • €€

10 De Zuiderkerk
Built 1603–11 by Hendrick de Keyser, painted by Monet in 1874. Climb to the top for stunning views of Amsterdam (see p42).

Left **Koninklijk Paleis** Right **View across Dam Square to the Nieuwe Kerk**

Nieuwe Zijde

DESPITE ITS NAME, THE NIEUWE ZIJDE (NEW SIDE), *together with the Oude Zijde, was at the centre of Amsterdam's early maritime settlement. From the boundary between the two districts, the Nieuwe Zijde extends west to the Singel. Its canal pattern once mirrored that of its neighbour, but over time it developed an entirely different character. The medieval city, with its wooden housing, was highly susceptible to fire, and much of the area was burnt down in 1452, necessitating extensive reconstruction. During the 19th century, most of its canals were filled in; the resulting thoroughfares, Damrak, Rokin and Nieuwendijk, are lively shopping streets, as is Kalverstraat, scene of a medieval market. Despite the changes, pockets of history survive – in the network of narrow 14th-century streets off Kalverstraat, the Begijnhof, the 17th-century orphanage that houses the Amsterdams Historisch Museum, and, at the heart of the district, Dam Square.*

18th-century monstrance, Museum Amstelring

🔟 Sights

1. Dam Square
2. Koninklijk Paleis
3. Nieuwe Kerk
4. Amsterdams Historisch Museum
5. Begijnhof
6. Museum Amstelring
7. Centraal Station
8. Beurs van Berlage
9. Allard Pierson Museum
10. Spui

Gilded cherub, Nieuwe Kerk

1 Dam Square
Amsterdam's main square is named after the dam on the River Amstel, around which the city grew. By the 17th century, it had become the focus of the Dutch trading empire *(see pp34-5)*.

2 Koninklijk Paleis
Supported by a staggering 13,659 wooden piles, Jacob van Campen's Classical building occupies one side of Dam Square. Designed as the *Stadhuis* (town hall), it was transformed into a Royal Palace in 1808 by King Louis Bonaparte. Although it is still used for official functions, such as the wedding reception of Crown Prince Willem-Alexander in February 2002 *(see p39)*, the present royal family live elsewhere. The interior is breathtaking *(see p34)*.

3 Nieuwe Kerk
Wealthy merchant banker Willem Eggert donated his orchard as a site for this Gothic church, as well as a large sum of money for its construction. It was consecrated to Our Lady and St Catherine, but has only ever been called the Nieuwe Kerk – to distinguish it from the Oude Kerk. When the town hall became the royal palace in the early 19th century *(see above)*, it was given the new, elevated title of national church of the Netherlands, and has been the setting for the coronation of every Dutch monarch since then.

4 Amsterdams Historisch Museum
An excellent place to start a visit to Amsterdam, this museum chronicles how a tiny fishing village on the Amstel river grew into one of the wealthiest and most beautiful cities in the world *(see pp24–7)*.

5 Begijnhof
A charming and secluded courtyard of houses surrounding a tranquil garden in the centre of the city, the Begijnhof was established in the 14th century as a sanctuary for a lay Catholic sisterhood *(see pp22–3)*.

6 Museum Amstelkring
This canal house turned museum, with its sober decoration and delightful secret Catholic church, plunges the visitor back into the Golden Age *(see pp20–1)*.

Amsterdams Historisch Museum collection

Centraal Station

Centraal Station

7 For many visitors, their experience of Amsterdam begins at Centraal Station, the transport hub of the city, where some 1,400 trains arrive and leave every day. It was built in the 1880s in Neo-Renaissance style by P J H Cuypers, who was also responsible for the startlingly similar Rijksmuseum *(see pp12–15)*, and A L van Gendt, designer of the Concertgebouw *(see p115)*. Before work on the building could start, three artificial islands had to be constructed and 8,600 wooden piles sunk to support them. The fact that the building blocked Amsterdammers' view of the sea caused much controversy at the time. The ornate red-brick façade depicts themes of travel, trade and city history, picked out in gold and other colours. If you have time to while away, the station restaurant Eerste Klas *(see p51)* serves full and light meals in a splendid Art Nouveau setting. ◊ *Stationsplein • Map P1 • 0900 9292*

Beurs van Berlage

8 The innovative Stock Exchange building was derided when it was unveiled in 1903, but is now considered a key work of the period and almost universally admired. Designed by the pioneer of Dutch modern architecture, H P Berlage, its functional lines are softened by ornamental ironwork and tiled mosaics. The Stock Exchange has now moved next door, and Beurs van Berlage is home to the Nederlands Philharmonic Orchestra. It is used for concerts and exhibitions, and contains a permanent display on the history of the Stock Exchange. Try to get a look at the amazingly light and spacious interior. ◊ *Damrak 277 • Map N2 • 020 530 4141 • www.beursvanberlage.nl • Open 11am–5pm Tue–Sun • Admission charge*

Allard Pierson Museum

9 Located in a stately Neo-Classical house built in the 1860s as a bank, this delightful small museum was named after the University of Amsterdam's first Professor of Classical Archaeology, and contains its archaeological collection. Fascinating exhibits conjure up vivid pictures of life in ancient civilizations; they include Egyptian mummies and sarcophagi, Coptic clothes, Cypriot jewellery, Greek geometric and red-figured pottery, Etruscan metalwork and Roman glassware and statuary. One of the museum's attractions is its size: even with an extra wing opened in 1994, it is

Amsterdam's Colonial Past

Acknowledged during the 17th century as the most powerful city in the Netherlands, Amsterdam turned its sights overseas. Expeditions established a spice trade out of Indonesia, and in 1602 the Dutch East India Company (VOC) was founded, followed in 1621 by the Dutch West India Company. Dutch colonies in Brazil and on Manhattan Island eventually succumbed, respectively, to Portuguese and English sea-power.

erfectly possible to see
verything in one visit. ® *Oude
urfmarkt 127 • Map N5 • 020 525 2556 •
www.uba.uva.nl/apm • Open 10am–5pm
ue–Fri, 1–5pm Sat, Sun & public hols •
dmission charge*

Spui
10 One of the most genial
laces in the city, this small
quare lined with cafés, bars and
ookshops is generally quiet
uring the winter, but in
ummer, it bursts into life at
unchtime and again in the
vening, when people spill out
nto the pavement from bars.
Cheek by jowl with university
uildings, Spui has traditionally
een a place where intellectuals
ather to drink and debate. There
s also a Friday book market.
During the Provo riots of the
960s *(see p39)*, the square was
he scene of political protests
nd demonstrations, during
which Carol Kneulman's twee
statue of an urchin, *Het Lieverdje*
Little Darling) was frequently
aubed with slogans. At No. 18,
Café Hoppe *(see p50)* is a
andmark brown café, in
usiness for more than 300
ears. ® *Map M5*

Het Lieverdje, Spui

A Day in the Nieuwe Zijde

Morning

Spend the morning in the **Amsterdams Historisch Museum** *(see pp24–7)*, although a morning is scarcely enough. When you feel like a break, leave the main building and head for the Kalverstraat entrance, where the café-restaurant David and Goliath is on your left. Make sure that you keep your ticket so that you can re-enter the museum without having to pay again. The end of the tour brings you to the excellent museum shop.

Rather than leaving by one of the exits, cut through the Civic Guards' Gallery to the **Begijnhof** *(see pp22–3)*, and while away some time in this secluded place. Come out of the Gedempte Begijnensloot entrance and turn the corner into **Spui**, where you might lunch at Café Hoppe *(see p50)* or Café Esprit (Spui 10).

Afternoon

After lunch, walk down Kalverstraat, the district's main shopping street, to Dam Square, where you could visit the **Koninklijk Paleis** as well as the **Nieuwe Kerk** *(see pp34–5)*. Then take a break among the tiny shops built into the buttresses of the church in Gravenstraat; at No.18, De Drie Fleschjes is one of the oldest *proeflokalen* (tasting houses), dating from 1650.

When you are revived, walk down Damrak past the **Beurs van Berlage** to finish your day at the **Centraal Station**, where you can hop on a tram back to your hotel.

Left **De Jaren** Right **Stereo Sushi**

TOP 10 Restaurants, Cafés and Bars

1 Green Planet
Bright, modern and full of greenery, this veggie café-restaurant is 90 per cent organic. Perfect for a drink, a quick snack or a hearty meal. ◉ *Spuistraat 122 • Map N2 • 020 625 8280 • €*

2 Henri Prouvin
In a pretty alley behind the Nieuwe Kerk, this dark, elegant bar serves a range of fine wines and champagnes, accompanied by soak-up snacks. ◉ *Gravenstraat 20 • Map N2*

3 Hoppe
Open since 1670, this historic brown café, with its lefty past and church pews, was a regular haunt of radical journalists, writers and intellectuals in the Provo-fuelled 1960s *(see p50)*.

4 De Jaren
Formerly a bank, cash is the only currency at this modern grand-café. Simple sandwiches and soups downstairs, delicious meals upstairs. The waterside terrace is the place to be in summer *(see p50)*.

5 Het Schuim
Art meets alcohol at this large, rustic-style bar, a popular hangout for students and creative types. Food served till 10pm. ◉ *Spuistraat 189 • Map M3*

6 Seymour Likely Lounge
With its huge "It's a bar" sign in the window, you couldn't fail to miss this hip drinking joint located in the city's "cool side". ◉ *Nieuwezijds Voorburgwal 250 • Map M*

7 Stereo Sushi
Service can be a little slow at this hip, imaginative sushi bar, so sip on sake while waiting for sushi, sashimi or even smoked eel. DJs spin late into the night. ◉ *Jonge Roelensteeg 4 • Map M3 • 020 777 3010 • €*

8 Supperclub
There's a decadent lounge bar in the basement of this painfully hip restaurant. Dress to impress if you want to get in. ◉ *Jonge Roelensteeg 21 • Map M3*

9 De Vijff Vlieghen
Elvis, Versace and John Wayne ate at this sprawling 300-seater restaurant. Each room has a theme, including the Rembrandt Room. Today it touts New Dutch cuisine, using mostly organic ingredients. ◉ *Spuistraat 294 • Map M4 • 020 530 4060 • €€€*

10 Villa Zeezicht
With wooded warmth and charm, this relaxed corner café has picture windows overlooking the wide cobbled bridge of the Singel. ◉ *Torensteeg 7 • Map M2*

Price Categories

For a three course meal for one with half a bottle of wine (or equivalent meal), taxes and extra charges.

€	under €20
€€	€20–€30
€€€	€30–€45
€€€€	€45–€60
€€€€€	over €60

De Bierkoning

🔟 Best of the Rest

1 Absinthe
DJs spin and you might too, after sampling the *La Fée Verte* (The Green Fairy), the controversial wormwood-infused hallucinogenic this late-opening lounge bar takes its name from. ◈ *Nieuwezijds Voorburgwal 171 • Map M3*

2 Al's Plaice
Authentic British fish'n'chips, complete with tabloids and lashings of tomato ketchup and brown sauce. ◈ *Nieuwendijk 10 • Map N1 • 020 427 4192 • €*

3 The American Book Center
Seven floors of books, magazines, newspapers and computer games. There are also art exhibitions, lectures and writers' workshops at the Treehouse annexe, a short walk away. ◈ *Kalverstraat 185 • Map M5*

4 De Bierkoning
"The Beer King" in the shadow of the Dam's Royal Palace has a fantastic range of beers – almost 1,000 of them – from all over the world. ◈ *Paleisstraat 125 • Map M3*

5 Housewives on Fire
An all-in-one store for a complete makeover. Funky hair styles and a good selection of clubbers' clothes. ◈ *Spuistraat 102 • Map N2*

6 P G C Hajenius
Dutchman Hajenius fulfilled his 1826 pipe dream, and his store is now one of Europe's most famous cigar houses. A must for all cigar connoisseurs, but worth a peek just for the art deco interior. ◈ *Rokin 92–6 • Map N3*

7 Pied-à-Terre
Spend an afternoon browsing the huge stock of travel guides and maps, while planning your next holiday or a short trip out of town. ◈ *Singel 393 • Map M5*

8 Puccini
Enjoy indescribably delicious home-made soups and imaginative sandwiches at this charming café erroneously calling itself an espressobar. Pricey but worth it, especially if you snag the corner couch. ◈ *Staalstraat 21 • Map P5*

9 De Still
Around 600 whiskies (most of them rare malts) are served at this specialist bar, which also runs an annual whisky festival. ◈ *Spuistraat 326 • Map M4*

10 Vrankrijk
Pop into the recently legalized bar of the city's most famous squat for a taste of Amsterdam's legendary squatting movement. ◈ *Spuistraat 216 • Map M4*

Left **Houseboat on Brouwersgracht** Right **De Star Hofje**

Western Canal Ring

FOR MANY, THE WESTERN CANAL RING *is the area of Amsterdam that perfectly encapsulates the city's relaxed yet stylish air. Construction of the Grachtengordel, Amsterdam's 17th-century ring of three fashionable canals (see p11), began here, with the marshy area just beyond reserved by city planner Hendrick Staets for workers and their unpalatable industries; Huguenot refugees who settled here – like others fleeing religious persecution – were said to have named it* jardin *(garden), later corrupted to Jordaan, and today it is one of Amsterdam's most fascinating – and bohemian – districts. Its narrow streets and oblique canals might seem random, but they followed the course of old paths and drainage ditches. North of the charming* Brouwersgracht *lies the recently revitalized district of Haarlemmerbuurt, and, further afield, the Western Islands, Bickerseiland, Prinseneiland and Realeneiland, created in the mid-17th century to provide much-needed warehousing.*

Huis met de Hoofden

🔟 Sights

1. Anne Frankhuis
2. Westerkerk
3. Theatremuseum
4. Huis met de Hoofden
5. Jordaan
6. Zon's Hofje and De Star Hofje
7. Noordermarkt
8. Brouwersgracht
9. Haarlemmerbuurt
10. Western Islands

1 Anne Frankhuis

Recently enlarged, this thought-provoking museum encompasses the *achterhuis*, secret hideout of Anne Frank and her family, as well as background information on the plight of Amsterdam's Jews and racial oppression *(see pp32-3)*.

2 Westerkerk

An exacting climb to the top of the soaring tower of Wester-kerk, a landmark close to the heart of every Amsterdammer, rewards you with a thrilling view of the city *(see p67)*. The church was designed by Hendrick de Keyser and completed in 1631. Its austere interior is unadorned, except for the ornate organ and its lively painted shutters. A memorial to Rembrandt reminds us that he was buried here, although the precise burial site is unknown. Outside the church, notice the poignant, diminutive statue of Anne Frank and Homomonument, the pink granite triangle which commemorates persecuted homo-sexuals. ⊗ *Prinsengracht 281. Map L2. 020 624 7766. www.westerkerk.nl • Church: open Apr–Sep: 11am–3pm Mon–Fri. Free • Tower: open Apr–Sep: guided tours every hour from 10am–4pm Mon–Sat. Admission charge*

3 Theatermuseum

Two fine buildings house the Theater-museum. Its entrance is at No. 168, the austere Neo-Classical White House designed in 1638 by Philips Vingboons and topped by Amsterdam's earliest neck gable. The museum extends into Nos 170–72, known as Bartolotti House, designed by

Theatermuseum

Hendrick de Keyser in 1617 with a contrastingly flamboyant Renaissance façade, its curved appearance cleverly reflecting the canal bend on which it stands. The frothy 18th-century stuccoed and painted interior of the White House is worth the visit alone. ⊗ *Herengracht 168 • Map L2 • 020 551 3300 • www.tin.nl • Open 11am–5pm Tue–Fri, 1–5pm Sat & Sun • Admission charge*

4 Huis met de Hoofden

An eye-catching extravaganza, the House with the Heads is named for the six heads on its elaborate step-gabled façade representing Classical gods – Apollo, Ceres, Mars, Minerva, Diana and Bacchus. Built in 1622 for a successful merchant, its Dutch Renaissance design is attributed to Hendrick de Keyser. Today it is occupied by the body in charge of Amsterdam's public monuments. The ground floor has scarcely changed. ⊗ *Keizersgracht 123 • Map L2 • Closed to the public except on Monumentendagen (see p70)*

Westerkerk

Hazenstraat, Jordaan

5 Jordaan

Quirky and characterful, with an intimate, easy-going atmosphere all its own, the Jordaan is a dense patch of small-scale streets and canals peppered with interesting shops and galleries, charming *hofjes* and inviting brown cafés. Bounded by Prinsengracht and Lijnbaansgracht to east and west, and Brouwersgracht and Looiersgracht to north and south, it was built for workers at the same time as the Grachtengordel *(see p11).* ⊗ *Map K3*

6 Zon's and De Star Hofjes

These two delightful *hofjes* are close to one another on Prinsengracht. At Zon's Hofje, a stone plaque depicting Noah's Ark is a clue that it was built on the site of a clandestine church known by that name. The De Star – officially Van Brienen – Hofje is named after a brewery that stood on this site. Merchant Jan Van Brienen is said to have built it in gratitude for his release from a vault in which he had accidently been locked. ⊗ *Zon's Hofje: Prinsengracht 159–171. Map D2. Open 10am–6pm Mon–Fri • De Star Hofje: Prinsengracht 89–133. Open 6am–6pm Mon-Fri, 6am–2pm Sat*

7 Noordermarkt

By the entrance to the Noorderkerk *(see p42)*, a still-flourishing Protestant church, a sculpture commemorates the *Jordaanoproer* (Jordaan riot) of 1934, in which seven people died during demonstrations against cuts in unemployment benefits. Today the tranquil surrounding square, a market site since 1627, comes to life during the Monday flea market and the Saturday bird market and *boerenmarkt*, selling organic produce. ⊗ *Map D2 • Flea market: 9am–1pm Mon • Boerenmarkt: 9am–4pm Sat*

8 Brouwersgracht

If you stand at the breezy junction of Brouwersgracht and Prinsengracht you will get terrific views in all directions, and a sense of the sea not far away. Today, Brouwersgracht, with its pretty bridges and picturesque houseboats, is a romantic delight, but a 17th-century brewery (*brouwer*) worker would be astonished to find that the spout-gabled warehouses of this once reeking industrial canal had now been converted into the smartest of private housing – particularly fine examples of which you can see at Nos 188–194. ⊗ *Map D1*

Hofjes

Secretive and intimate, Amsterdam's *hofjes* – almshouses for the needy built by wealthy merchants in the 17th and 18th centuries – are part of the city's charm. Unobtrusive street entrances lead to pretty houses (sometimes still used for their original purpose) around a flower-filled garden or courtyard. Visitors are usually admitted, but they are asked to respect residents' privacy.

9 Haarlemmerbuurt

In recent times, the bustling streets of this stalwart residential neighbourhood have seen the arrival of all manner of shops, mixing bric-a-brac with *haute couture*, New Age with funky furniture and specialist food with local groceries. On Haarlemmerstraat is Westindisch Huis, once the headquarters of the Dutch West India Company *(see p45)*. To the west is Haarlemmerpoort, a gateway – now converted into flats – built in 1840 for the entry of William II. Beyond it lies peaceful Westerpark, and Westergasfabriek, former gasworks turned arts centre. ⬥ *Map D1*

10 Western Islands

Despite being very much part of the city, the man-made Western Islands have a remote, bracing quality. Comprising Bickerseiland, Prinseneiland and Realeneiland, they were created in the early 17th century to accommodate shipyards and warehouses. In recent years, large-scale development has taken place, and modern housing now co-exists in harmony with white wooden drawbridges. Don't miss Zandhoek on Realeneiland, with its row of charming 17th-century houses, or atmospheric Prinseneiland with its boatyard and old shuttered warehouses. ⬥ *Map D1*

Boatyard, Prinseneiland

Exploring the Western Canal Ring

Morning

🕐 Beat the queues and be first to arrive at the **Anne Frankhuis** *(see pp32–3)*, which opens at 9am. Afterwards, you could take a contemplative walk along Prinsengracht to the Western Islands, perhaps first climbing the tower of **Westerkerk** *(see p91)*. On the way, drop in on two peaceful *hofjes*, **Zon's** and **De Star** *(see facing page)*. For refreshment, visit
☕ Papeneiland, a tiny brown café founded in 1642, at the junction of Prinsengracht and Brouwersgracht.

On the **Western Islands**, stroll round Prinseneiland and along Zandhoek on Realeneiland, where you could lunch very well at
🍴 De Gouden Reael (Zandhoek 14). If you are with children, visit Dierencapel, the children's farm on Bickerseiland.

Afternoon

En route to the Jordaan, hardened shoppers will first want to stop in
🛍 **Haarlemmerbuurt**, with its mix of shops, both smart and tatty. Don't miss a peak at over-the-top Café Dulac (Haarlemmerstraat 118), and the world's narrowest restaurant, De Groene Lanteerne (Haarlemmerstraat 43).

Spend a couple of hours exploring the endlessly picturesque **Jordaan**, then join today's breed of young Jordaanese in one of the trendy cafés around Noordermarkt – Finch or
☕ Proust, or the wildly kitsch Café Nol in Westerstraat. If it's dinner time, head for
🍴 De Reiger *(see p51)*, the locals' favourite *eetcafé*.

Left **'t Smalle** Right **Finch**

🔟 Bars and Cafés

1 't Arend's Nest
Over 130 types of Dutch beer (many from small, local breweries) are served at this specialist bar – with several on tap. On the last Sunday of each month, sample 10 different kinds in their informal tasting sessions. ◈ *Herengracht 90 • Map M1*

2 Duende
Release the inner gypsy in this small, busy tapas bar in the Jordaan. Authentic atmosphere, value for money, and regular live music. Olé! ◈ *Lindengracht 62 • Map C2 • 020 420 6692 • €€*

3 Finch
This small but popular watering-hole on the edge of a scenic square can get decidedly crowded. In summer, the hip local clientele spills out onto the square. ◈ *Noordermarkt 5 • Map D2*

4 P96
This peaceful bar opens around 8pm in the evenings and stays open later than most. The premises extend in the summer to an outdoors terrace on a fairy-lit barge. ◈ *Prinsengracht 96 • Map L1*

5 De Reiger
A stylish and popular brown bar-restaurant for those with discerning taste-buds. Not your usual "pub grub" *(see p51)*.

6 Sassoon
An unusual and arty experience is guaranteed at this split-level bar. Unique and quintessentially Amsterdam. ◈ *Marnixstraat 79 • Map C1*

7 't Smalle
Originally a liquor distillery, this split-level brown bar is now a discerning wine-café. A must-see. ◈ *Egelantiersgracht 12 • Map L1*

8 Sound Garden
Don't let the tattoos, piercings and grunge factor put you off. This huge bar has a great atmosphere and some unusual beers on tap, too. ◈ *Marnixstraat 164–166 • Map J3*

9 Tabac
Tabac used to be a brown café but has recently succumbed to the lounge trend. Locals notice, visitors may not. ◈ *Brouwersgracht 101 • Map D2*

10 Vandenberg
A lesbian-run bar-restaurant located on a wide street that was once a canal famous for its eel-baiting contests. The 1886 Eel Riot (in which 26 died and 136 were wounded) took place here. You won't, however, find eel on the menu – it's vegetarian. ◈ *Lindengracht 95 • Map D2 • 020 622 2716 • €*

Price Categories

For a three course meal for one with half a bottle of wine (or equivalent meal), taxes and extra charges.

€	under €20
€€	€20–€30
€€€	€30–€45
€€€€	€45–€60
€€€€€	over €60

Spanjer & Van Twist

10 Restaurants

1 Balraj
The sister of Beatrix, Queen of the Netherlands, is a regular diner at this well-priced restaurant offering some of the best Indian food in town. ◈ *Haarlemmerdijk 28 • Map D1 • 020 625 1428 • €€*

2 De Belhamel
The charm and ambience of this canalside restaurant more than make up for the somewhat variable quality of the food. ◈ *Brouwersgracht 60 • Map D2 • 020 622 1095 • €€€*

3 De Bolhoed
Undoubtedly one of the most charming restaurants in the area. Delicious, well-priced vegetarian (and vegan) food with a wicked dessert selection *(see p61).*

4 Christophe
Algerian-born Jean-Christophe Royer started out washing dishes. Today he's one of the finest chefs in the Netherlands: his Mediterranean establishment has a coveted Michelin star. *Trés cher.* ◈ *Leliegracht 46 • Map L2 • 020 625 0807 • €€€€€*

5 Foodism
A great little place tucked away in this narrow street. Delicious, healthy food, including a wide range of vegetarian options. ◈ *Oude Leliestraat 8 • Map L2 • 020 427 5103 • €*

6 New Deli
This hip, white, minimalist establishment serves a Japanese-inspired menu alongside sandwiches and salads. ◈ *Haarlemmerstraat 73 • Map D2 • 020 626 2755 • €€*

7 Sjaalman
A trendy Thai that looks across the canal to the Westerkerk. A tad expensive, but the food is authentic. ◈ *Prinsengracht 178 • Map K2 • 020 620 2440 • €€*

8 Spanjer & Van Twist
The perfect place to rest those weary feet. Hole yourself up for the afternoon in the second-floor window seat. ◈ *Leliegracht 60 • Map L2 • 020 620 2440 • €€*

9 Toscanini
Despite its quiet location and deceptive size (it's huge inside), this superb Italian restaurant gets quickly booked up. The cooks create delicious dishes from an open kitchen. ◈ *Lindengracht 75 • Map C2 • 020 623 2813 • €€€*

10 De Vliegende Schotel
Slow service, but infinitely worth it for the huge portions of delicious vegetarian food. House wine is the only alcohol served. ◈ *Nieuwe Leliestraat 162 • Map K2 • 020 625 2041 • €*

Left **Donald E Jongejans** Right **Mechanisch Speelgoed**

Shopping

1 Back Beat
Jools Holland and even Mick Jagger have popped into this new and second-hand record/CD shop specializing in jazz, soul, funk and R&B. Rare collector's items to be had. ◈ *Egelantiersstraat 19 • Map L1*

2 De Belly
Unable to wait for Saturday's organic market? Then head to this friendly organic store. Pulses, grains, candles, soaps, fresh fruit and vegetables, plus a good selection of wine and beer. ◈ *Nieuwe Leliestraat 174 • Map K2*

3 Big Shoe
Fashionable footwear for folk with big feet. ◈ *Leliegracht 12 • Map L2*

4 De Blue Gold Fish
The staff can be a little barmy at the best of times, but persevere and you should be able to find an unusual gift at this eccentric arts and crafts shop. ◈ *Rozengracht 17 • Map K3*

5 Donald E Jongejans
Vintage frames specialist selling a fascinating selection of eyewear dating from the 1800s onwards. If it's shut, just check out the window display. ◈ *Noorderkerkstraat 18 • Map D2*

6 Exota
One of a handful of typically Jordaan boutiques in this area – with a trendier edge than most. ◈ *Nieuwe Leliestraat 32 • Map K2*

7 Kitsch Kitchen
Ample to spice up your kitchen and accessorize the cooks. Pop across the nearby Rozengracht to number 183, where "Kitsch Kitchen Kids" has a range for the little people. ◈ *Eerste Bloemdwarsstraat 21–23 • Map K*

8 Mechanisch Speelgoed
A fascinating, nostalgia-inducing collection of mechanica toys and good old-fashioned children's playthings. Simply put: life before Gameboy. ◈ *Westerstraat 67 • Map D2*

9 Pasta Panini
A fabulous Italian deli. Grea for freshly-filled ciabattas at lunchtime or hand-made pasta for supper. Plus a tantalizing range of cookies, soup, sauces and wine. ◈ *Rozengracht 82 • Map K*

10 Simon Levelt
There are a staggering 160 type of tea and around 2 types of coffee to choose from in this pleasant, aromatic store. The company has been importing the stuff since 1817 ◈ *Prinsengracht 180 • Map K2*

Left **GO Cantina** Right **Pancake Bakery**

Best of the Rest

1 Avondverkoop Dolf
In a town which doesn't quite have the 24/7 American mentality, this late-night store can be a Godsend – even if it is a little pricey. General groceries and a good range of alchohol. ◈ *Willemstraat 79 • Map D1*

2 Gambit
A whisky-laced hot chocolate in one hand, and a bishop in the other ... when the heavens open, hole up in this delightful chess café for a few hours and checkmate your opponent. ◈ *Bloemgracht 20 • Map K2*

3 't Geveltje
Beginners and pros jam together in the Jordaan's famous jazz bar for musicians and jazz aficionados alike. Pros play every Friday. Closed Saturdays and Sundays. ◈ *Bloemgracht 170 • Map J2*

4 GO Cantina
Every so often a dining table is set up within this art gallery space and GO goes gourmet. ◈ *GO Gallery, Prinsengracht 4 • Map L1*

5 Greenwoods
Australian-run, typically English tearoom-style café that serves great breakfasts and high teas. Service can be painfully slow, but worth the wait. ◈ *Singel 103 • Map M1*

6 Jordaan Festival
The "Jordaaners" are fiercely proud of the accordion-laden oompah songs unique to this area. Over one weekend mid-September, outdoor stages are set up on this filled-in canal, and the beer and bellowing flow freely. ◈ *Elandsgracht • Map K4*

7 De Koophandel
Unusual for Amsterdam, a late-night bar, on one of the prettier, quieter canals in the Jordaan. ◈ *Bloemgracht 49 • Map K2*

8 Pancake Bakery
Although unashamedly touristy, you could do a lot worse than this restaurant in a former 17th-century warehouse named "Hope" to sample the local fare. ◈ *Prinsengracht 191 • Map L1*

9 Paradox
A paradox in itself, this coffeeshop shows few traces of serving "the herb". Fresh fruit and veg shakes, healthy food and a bright interior make it a perfect place for breakfast or lunch. ◈ *Eerste Bloemstraat 2 • Map K2*

10 Small World
Simply the best quick-stop in town for sandwiches, carrot cake and other delicious offerings. Eat in at the counter or take away. ◈ *Binnen Oranjestraat 14 • Map D1*

Left **Vintage robots for sale at the Looier Kunst an Antiekcentrum** Right **Leidseplein at night**

Central Canal Ring

A MSTERDAM'S THREE GREAT CANALS, *Herengracht, Keizersgracht and Prinsengracht, are at their most impressive in this central section of the Grachtengordel (see p11), which culminates in the stretch known as the Golden Bend, where the wealthiest Amsterdammers built stately houses in the 1660s. Designed and decorated by the best architects of the day, such a Philips Vingboons, the mansions built here were often twice the width of standard canal houses. Nowadays, many of these buildings are occupied by institutions. In contrast, the intimate cross-streets that run between the three canals, known as De Negen Straatjes (The Nine Streets) enticingly display th city's talent for creative retail. Another magnet for shoppers is Metz & Co, which provides a bird's-eye view of the whole area from its top-floor café.*

Cutting through this elegant district is the main thoroughfare, Leidsestraat, which culminates in the brash and lively entertainment hub, Leidse-plein. Architectural highlights include the Paleis van Justitie and the American Hotel.

Cupola, Metz & Co

🔟 Sights

1. Golden Bend
2. Bijbels Museum
3. Singel
4. Metz & Co
5. Leidsegracht
6. Negen Straatjes
7. Felix Meritis Building
8. Looier Kunst en Antiekcentrum
9. Leidseplein
10. American Hotel

odel of Temple Mount, Jerusalem, jbels Museum

1 Golden Bend

So named because of the oncentration of wealth amongst s first residents, this stretch of he Herengracht between ijzelstraat and Leidsestraat feels rand but bland, unless you pick ut eye-catching details as you troll. Look out for Louis XIV-tyle No. 475, said to be msterdam's most beautiful ouse; and No. 476, elegantly estyled in the 1730s and topped vith an eagle. No. 497 is open to he public, but you have to like ats: it's the Kattenkabinet, a nique museum devoted to cats art. Be careful not to trip over ne of the many feline attend-nts. ◈ *Kattenkabinet: Herengracht 97 • Map M6 • 020 626 5378 • www.kattenkabinet nl • Open am–2pm Mon-Fri, 1–5pm Sat & Sun • dmission charge*

2 Bijbels Museum

Far lovelier than the Golden end is the stretch of Heren-racht between Huidenstraat and eidsestraat, particularly Nos 64–70, four houses built by hilips Vingboons in 1662. Two of em house the Bible Museum, here apart from biblical arti-cts you can admire the early-8th-century interior. ◈ *Heren-racht 366 • Map L5 • 020 624 2436 • www.bijbelsmuseum.nl • Open Jam–5pm Mon-Sat, 1–5pm Sun • dmission charge*

3 Singel

Often overlooked by tourists, Singel is an excellent canal for a stroll, measuring just over 1.6 km (1 mile). Once a fortified moat, it marks the boundary between the densely packed medieval city and its more spacious 17th-century extension. Its central section is graced by the elegant Neo-Gothic Krijtberg church with its ornate interior *(see p43)*. Take a look, too, at Singel 288, with gorgeous Rococo façade, and at Torensluis, a bridge wide enough for café tables and a domineer-ing statue of the writer Multatuli *(see p47)*. ◈ *Map N1*

4 Metz & Co

The great attraction of this ponderous late-19th-century building (apart, of course, from the five floors of luxury goods on sale) is its sixth-floor cupola and café, with superb views of the canal ring below. Originally built for an insurance company in 1891, it was taken over by Metz & Co in 1908. Gerrit Rietveld added his splendid glass cupola in 1933. In 1973, Liberty of London bought the business, renovated the building and commissioned Cees Dam to design the sixth-floor café. ◈ *Leidsestraat 34–36 • Map L6 • 020 520 7020 • Open 11am–6pm Mon, 9:30am–6pm Tue–Sat, noon–5pm Sun*

Torensluis bridge, Singel

5 Leidsegracht

For dream canal houses in pristine condition, look no further than sophisticated Leidsegracht, one of the city's most sought-after addresses. At Herengracht 394, on the corner with Leidsegracht, notice the fine wall plaque depicting characters from a medieval legend – the four *Heemskinderen* on their horse Beyaart. Another plaque, at No. 39, shows Cornelis Lely, who drew up the original plans for draining the Zuiderzee. ⚑ *Map K6*

6 Negen Straatjes

Nestling in the centre of the canal ring are these three parallel rows of cross-streets bordered by Singel and Prinsengracht to east and west, and Raadhuisstraat and Leidsegracht to north and south. Known collectively as the Nine Streets, these charming, largely car-free roads were once a centre for the leather trade. Today they are packed with amusing, imaginative and sometimes eccentric shops like De Witte Tandenwinkel, devoted to toothbrushes *(see p104)*. In Gasthuismolensteeg, don't miss the Brilmuseum at No. 7, an enchanting museum and shop devoted to spectacles old and new (open noon–5pm Wed–Sat). ⚑ *Map L4*

Houseboats

Around 2,500 houseboats are called "home" in Amsterdam, but it was only after World War II, when there was a severe housing shortage, that they become popular. Though linked to the electricity and water supplies, they use the canals (which are flushed out nightly) for sewage disposal. Visit the Woonbootmuseum (Houseboat Museum) opposite Prinsengracht 296 to find out more.

Felix Meritis Building

7 Felix Meritis Building

The splendid Neo-Classical façade of this building comes as a surprise on gabled Keizersgracht. Designed in 1787 by Jacob Otten Husly as a science and arts centre (the name Felix Meritis means "happiness through merit"), it flourished until the late 19th century. Later, it became headquarters of the Dutch Communist Party (CPN), and in the 1970s was home to the avant-garde Shaffy Theatre Company. Today, the Felix Meritis Society has been revived, and its arts complex and Summer University courses ensure that it is always humming. ⚑ *Keizersgracht 324 • Map L4 • 020 623 1311*

8 Looier Kunst en Antiekcentrum

If the smart shops of the Spiegelkwartier *(see p112)* are too expensive and rarified, try searching for more affordable antiques – everything from vintage toys to glass, lace and Delftware – in this warren of stalls occupying a vast network of ground-floor rooms in a block of houses near the Looiersgracht (tanners' canal). Taken together, this is the largest collection of art and antiques in the Netherlands. The stall-holders have a lively community spirit, hosting bridge sessions which are open to all. ⚑ *Elandsgracht 109 • Map J5 • Open 11am–5pm Sat–Thu*

Leidseplein

The city's tourist hub. Sophisticated it is not, tacky and
in (and, at night, often raucous) it is, especially in summer, when buskers and street performers, from family pop groups to lone fire-eaters, keep the milling throngs amused. Despite its rambling, dog-leg shape, Leidseplein is a natural gathering place, packed with fast food stalls, cafés and smoking coffee shops. Nightspots De Melkweg, Paradiso, and Holland Casino are close at hand, while for a more reflective diversion you can play chess on a giant outdoor chessboard in adjacent Max Euweplein, or stroll in the tiny Leidsebos park. ◎ Map C5

American Hotel

Leidseplein's most famous landmark is this one-off Dutch interpretation of Art Nouveau by Willem Kromhout (1902), which retold the Amsterdam School of architecture. Only the exterior is of interest: the interior is as bland as any other chain hotel (in this case, Crowne Plaza). The exception is the hotel's famous Café Americain, with its stained-glass windows and glass parasol lampshades. The literati who once inhabited it may have disappeared, but it's a welcome haven from the rigours of Leidseplein. ◎ Map C5

Looking towards the American Hotel

Exploring the Central Canal Ring

Morning

This compact area is focused on Amsterdam's most famous canals, so why not start the day with a canal tour. Amsterdam Canal Cruises start and end on Singelgracht, opposite the Heineken Brewery. From here, it's a short walk to **Leidseplein** and welcome refreshment at the **Café Americain**.

Leaving the hubbub of Leidseplein, walk along Prinsengracht (passing the Paleis van Justitie, once the city orphanage) to elegant **Leidsegracht**. If there's time, investigate the antiques market, **Looier**, in Elandsgracht. For lunch, try brown cafés Van Puffelen or Het Molenpad, or designer hang-out Het Land van Walem (see p102).

Afternoon

Plunge into the **Negen Straatjes** for some serious shopping in its frivolous shops. You may not be able to resist the cakes and chocolate on offer at salon de thé Pompadour (see p104). Pop into the Woonbootmuseum, moored on Prinsengracht opposite Elandsgracht, to marvel at how a bargeman and his family could have lived in such a tiny space. Then cross to Herengracht, which you will have seen earlier from the water, and stroll along, admiring its architectural gems around the **Bijbels Museum** and **Golden Bend** (see p99). If it's before 6pm (9pm on Thu, 5pm on Sun), end the afternoon with a bird's eye view of your day's exploration from the sixth-floor café at **Metz & Co** (see p99).

Around Town – Central Canal Ring

For more on canal tours See pp10 and 136

Left **The Bar With No Name** Right **Van Puffelen**

Top 10 Bars

1 De Admiraal
One of the smarter *proeflokaalen* (tasting houses) in the city – and unlike the rest, it closes late. Collapse on the couches and knock back the potent liquors and *jenever*. ◎ *Herengracht 319 • Map L4*

2 The Bar With No Name
Known to the locals as Wolvenstraat, this 1970s-style lounge bar-restaurant is the haunt of young advertising darlings and other affluent beings. Open from breakfast to bedtime, it serves imaginative sandwiches, soup and pan-Asian cuisine. ◎ *Wolvenstraat 23 • Map L4 • 020 320 0843 • €€*

3 Kamer 401
Tasteful 1960s lounge bar done out in blacks and greys. Early in the evening, a pre-theatre crowd dines here. Later, trendy young things take over. Note: it's a tad expensive and cash only. ◎ *Marnixstraat 401 • Map K6*

4 Het Land van Walem
One of the city's original designer bars, this was the creation of renowned Dutch architect, Gerrit Rietveld. Inside, it's bright and minimalist; outside, there are charming terraces. ◎ *Keizersgracht 449 • Map L6*

5 Lux
Split-level, late-opening designer bar. DJs spin every night. ◎ *Marnixstraat 403 • Map K6*

6 Het Molenpad
A charming brown bar between the city's main library and the Leidsestraat – equally suitable for bookworms and the shopped-out. ◎ *Prinsengracht 653 • Map K5 • 020 625 9680 • €€*

7 Morlang
Modern, minimalist space next door to Land van Walem. Impressive menu. ◎ *Keizersgracht 451 • Map L6 • 020 625 2681 • €€*

8 Saarein II
Once an infamous women-only bar, now men are welcome. Quiet during the week, rowdy at weekends. Pool table, good bar food. ◎ *Elandsstraat 119 • Map K4*

9 Van Puffelen
The rich and beautiful flock to this elegant haunt – the biggest brown bar in town. ◎ *Prinsengracht 377 • Map K3 • 020 62 6270 • €€*

10 De Zotte
This Belgian bar (appropriately named "Drunken Fool") has a huge range of beers. Delicious food helps soak it all up. ◎ *Raamstraat 29 • Map K 020 626 8694 • €€€*

agamama

🔟 Restaurants

1 Blakes
Save this restaurant located Anoushka Hempel's upmarket otel for a special occasion. The od is a fusion of French and astern – highly creative, but at a ost *(see p144).* 🗷 €€€€€

2 Bojo
Inexpensive, informal and donesian – head here after ost of the city's restaurants ave gone to bed. 🗷 *Lange idsedwarsstraat 49–51 • Map D5 • 0 622 7434 • €*

3 Goodies
A culinary delight in the art of the Nine Streets. ealthy soups, salads and ndwiches by day; the perfect sta by night. 🗷 *Huidenstraat 9 • ap L5 • 020 625 6122 • €*

4 Los Pilones
This Mexican cantina is small, t size isn't everything. Savour e authentic home cooking, tween slams of tequila. 🗷 *Kerk- aat 63 • Map L6 • 020 320 4651 • €€*

5 Noa
Canalside chic is nvented at this w York-style unge bar, with ampagne, cocktails d couches to kick ck in. The food is , but sometimes misses. 🗷 *Leidse- cht 84 • Map K6 • 020 5 0802 • €€€*

6 Metz & Co
The views at this prestigious department store's restaurant are spectacular; the food less so *(see p99).* 🗷 €€

7 Nomads
This late-night restaurant is the ultimate in decadent dining. Kick off your shoes and lounge on mattresses while food is served to you from bronze platters. DJs enhance the Arabian experience at weekends. 🗷 *Rozengracht 133 • Map J3 • 020 344 6401 • €€€€*

8 Rakang
Totally authentic Thai; one of the best of its kind in the city. Those in the know load up at their cheaper, equally delicious take- away next door. 🗷 *Elandsgracht 29–31 • Map K4 • 020 620 9551 • €€€*

9 TamTam
An exclusive new restaurant, exclusively priced. On some nights, you might catch celebrity chef Jaymz Pool in the kitchen. Cash only. 🗷 *Prinsengracht 381 • Map K3 • 020 612 0960 • €€€*

🔟 Wagamama
Fast food, slow service – but you could do worse for a quick lunch. Don't miss the king-size chess action taking place on the giant board outside. 🗷 *Max Euweplein 10 • Map C5 • 020 528 7778 • €*

Around Town – Central Canal Ring

Price Categories		
For a three course meal for one with half a bottle of wine (or equivalent meal), taxes and extra charges.	**€**	under €20
	€€	€20–€30
	€€€	€30–€45
	€€€€	€45–€60
	€€€€€	over €60

Left **Pontifex** Right **Fifties-Sixties**

🔟 Shopping (Nine Streets)

1 Bakkerij Paul Année
Where can you find the best bread in Amsterdam? At this organic baker's outlet, selling a delicious range of wholemeal bread and croissants, pizza, tofu *broodjes* and sugar-free oatcakes. ◈ *Runstraat 25 • Map K5*

2 Fifties-Sixties
Accessorize your house with this kitsch selection of designer toasters, lava lamps and lighting from – you guessed it – the 1950s and 60s. ◈ *Huidenstraat 13 • Map L5*

3 De Kaaskamer
For cheese with a capital C, try "The Cheese Chamber", where there are over 200 different kinds of one of Holland's best exports. If it isn't here, it probably doesn't exist. ◈ *Runstraat 7 • Map K5*

4 d Pharmacy
If you need a mousetrap wall-light, or perhaps a double coffee cup (espresso one way up, regular the other), then this is the place. ◈ *Wolvenstraat 14 • Map L4*

5 Pompadour
You can pile on the calories just staring at the window-display of this chique chocolaterie. Sadly, all you'll burn here is a hole in your wallet. Try the famous home-made chocolates or exquisite tarts. ◈ *Huidenstraat 12 • Map L5*

6 Pontifex
This tiny waxworks gives Madame Tussauds a run for the money, with a colourful range of candles of every type imaginable. Adjoining are the premises of the rather spooky doll doctor, Kramer. ◈ *Reestraat 20 • Map K3*

7 Razzmatazz
A must for a designer collection ranging from Vivienne Westwood to Dexter Wong – plus accessories, and information on clubs and parties. ◈ *Wolvenstraat • Map L4*

8 What's Cooking
At this kitsch and colourful culinary store you'll find everything from jam spoons and tablecloth saris to olive oil and iced tea – plus gadgets and gismos to suit every cook's pocket. ◈ *Reestraat 16 • Map L3*

9 De Witte Tandenwinkel
A veritable ode to the tooth, this shop specializes in every shape or size of toothbrush imaginable, and is sure to take your (bad) breath away. Mouthy Mick Jagger has even dropped by. ◈ *Runstraat 5 • Map L5*

10 Zipper
Immaculately displayed vintage second-hand clothes and accessories. ◈ *Huidenstraat 7 • Map L5*

Left **Frozen Fountain** Right **Melkweg**

10 Best of the Rest

1 Bagel & Beans
American-style freshly-baked cookies and cheesecake, freshly-squeezed juices and (rare in Amsterdam) decent-sized cups of coffee. ⊗ *Keizersgracht 504 • Map L5*

2 Ben & Jerry's
Forget the nearby Häagen-Dazs parlour – ice cream never tasted this good. ⊗ *Leidsestraat 90 • Map K6*

3 Frozen Fountain
Arguably, Amsterdam's most important designer store and exhibition space for furniture and household products. A revered international reputation for its cutting-edge designs and fresh talent makes it a must-see. ⊗ *Prinsengracht 629 • Map K5*

4 Urban Home & Garden Tours
Garden designer André Ancion gives English-language walking tours delving behind the façades of some of the city's most impressive canal houses. It ends with a very civilized lunch or afternoon tea. ⊗ *020 688 1243*

5 Melkweg
This former milk factory now churns out live music. Plus there's a cinema, theatre, gallery, café-bar, upstairs bar and mint-sized video room (see p54).

6 Paradiso
One of Amsterdam's best-loved live music spots. Velvet Underground, Buzzcocks and Macy Gray have all played here. The intimate upstairs hall often has unknowns before they go big. ⊗ *Weteringschans 6-8 • Map C5*

7 Hotel Pulitzer
Opera brunches take place on the last Sunday of the month in the "Garden Room" of this prestigious hotel. In August, the hampers and champagne come out in full force, when a floating stage is set up out front for the unmissable Grachtenfestival's open-air classical concert. ⊗ *Prinsengracht 315–331 • Map K3*

8 Design is Dead
But not here. A fantastic selection of trendy and original innovations, reasonably priced. You can't walk past without going in. ⊗ *Leidsestraat 61 • Map L6*

9 Sound of the Fifties
A unique record shop stocking rare and collectable vinyl from the 1950s. ⊗ *Prinsengracht 669 • Map K6*

10 La Tertulia
A mother and daughter team run this bright, split-level canalside coffeeshop. Perfect for first-timers. ⊗ *Prinsengracht 312 • Map K5*

Left **Munttoren** Right **Dray horses at the Heineken Experience**

Eastern Canal Ring

BEGUN IN THE EARLY 17TH CENTURY, *the Grachtengordel (see p11) was extended further east to reach the Amstel in the 1660s, making new plots of land available for wealthy merchants to build their luxurious if sober town houses. Among the highlights of the area are two such patrician mansions, the Museum Van Loon and the Museum Willet-Holthuysen. Medieval Amsterdam is recalled at the Munttoren, whose base was once part of the Regulierspoort, a gate in the city wall; by contrast, you can see the modern city in full swing in lively Rembrandtplein, formerly a butter market.*

There are diverse opportunities for shopping among the antiques of the Spiegelkwartier, at the colourful Bloemenmarkt, and at vibrant Albert Cuypmarkt; or you could catch a movie at Abraham Tuschinski's extraordinary 1921 cinema, now lovingly restored and offering six screens. And to refresh the parts that other beers may or may not be able to reach, you can visit the original Heineken Brewery for a guided tour and a free beer.

Tuschinski Theatre

Sights

1. Museum Van Loon
2. Museum Willet-Holthuysen
3. Amstel River
4. Rembrandtplein
5. Tuschinski Theatre
6. Munttoren
7. Bloemenmarkt
8. Spiegelkwartier
9. Heineken Experience
10. Albert Cuypmarkt

1 Museum Van Loon

A chance to see inside a private canal house, whose grand yet approachable 18th-century interior recreates a bygone age *(see pp30–31)*.

2 Museum Willet-Holthuysen

Though it lacks the lived-in feel of the Museum Van Loon, this 17th-century canal house has its own special atmosphere. An air of stiff formality tinged with melancholy pervades its stately rooms: the Ballroom; the Blue Room, reserved for the men of the house, with painted ceiling by Jacob de Wit; the glittering Dining Room; and the delicate Garden Room, with views over the formal garden. The collect-ions of its last owners, Sandrina Holthuysen and her husband, Abraham Willet, are displayed throughout – paintings, glass, ceramics, silver. It was the widowed Sandrina who left the house and its contents to the city. She died a lonely death in 1885, trying to keep up appearances in a house by then overrun with cats. ⬧ *Herengracht 605 • Map P6 • 020 523 1870 • www.ahm.nl • Open 10am–5pm Mon–Fri, 11am–5pm Sat & Sun • Admission charge*

Museum Willet-Holthuysen

Magere Brug

3 Amstel River

No visit to Amsterdam is complete without a walk along the banks of the Amstel, the river whose mouth spawned a fishing settlement in the 12th century *(see p38)*. In 1222 the river was dammed, and Amsterdam turned from fishing to trade – the beginning of its expansion. Commercial barges still ply the river, passing Blauwbrug (Blue Bridge), inspired by the *belle époque* Pont Alexandre III in Paris, the much-loved Magere Brug *(see p11)*, and the Amstelsluizen (sluice gates), which help to pump millions of gallons of fresh water into the canals to keep them from stagnating. ⬧ *Map P5*

4 Rembrandtplein

This former butter market has what you might call a split personality. In its centre is a 19th-century statue of Rembrandt set in a tranquil garden, but around its sides are neon-lit, low-brow and – at night – high-octane bars and cafés, packed with Amsterdammers and visitors alike. This is a great place for an early evening drink; you might choose grand cafés Schiller *(see p113)* and De Kroon *(see p50)*, as popular at the turn of the 20th century as they are now. ⬧ *Map N6*

5 Tuschinski Theatre

Amsterdam's – perhaps the world's – most elaborate cinema was the extraordinary creation of a driven, self-made Jewish tailor from Poland. Obsessed by film and the belief that it could change lives, he masterminded a vast team of craftsmen and conjured the cinema, in 1921, in a slum known as Devil's Corner. He was later to perish in Auschwitz, but his wonderful creation – loosely Art Nouveau, but termed Tuschinski Style for its unique mixture of influences – lives on. In 2002 it reopened, after a multi-million dollar renovation. In the process, hitherto unknown paintings of Vogue-style ladies were uncovered, and the theatre has been returned to its former breathtaking glory. Buy a ticket for Screen One to admire the main theatre before the lights go down. Reguliersbreestraat 26–28 • Map N6

6 Munttoren

Take a close look at the Mint Tower (it was briefly used as the city mint in 1673). Its bottom half is the remnant of a gate in the medieval city wall. When the gate burned down in 1618, Hendrick de Keyser slapped one

---

Flower Power

The Dutch adore flowers, particularly tulips. They are everywhere, on window boxes, in houses, in shops and markets. You can buy bulbs at the Bloemenmarkt, visit the vast flower auction at Aalsmeer and the spring spectacle at Keukenhof (see p72-3), and cycle through the bulbfields near Leiden. But you won't find the mythical black tulip: it doesn't exist, though breeders are very getting close to it.

Blooms at the Bloemenmarkt

of his clock towers (see p42) on top of the remains. The carillon of 1699 rings every 15 minutes. Today, there is a gift shop on the ground floor. Map N5

7 Bloemenmarkt

Undoubtedly one of Amsterdam's most picturesque sights, the flower market is a magnet for tourists. There are local shoppers too, buying armfuls for their houses, while visitors arrange for bulbs to be mailed home. Vendors once sailed up the Amstel from their nurseries to this spot on the Singel, selling their wares directly from their boats. Nowadays the stalls are still floating, though you wouldn't know it as they feel firmly fixed. Map M5

8 Spiegelkwartier

In the late 19th century, specialist antique dealers with an eye for an opportunity began to set up shop on Nieuwe Spiegelstraat, leading to the newly opened Rijksmuseum. There are more than 80 of them in the area now, making it a sparkling, elegant place in which to stroll. Content yourself with looking longingly at the gleaming displays of antique furniture, porcelain and glass, or treat yourself to a faded old Delft tile for just a few euros from Kramer (see p112). Map D5

9 Heineken Experience

The biggest draw to Heineken's former brewery, which ceased production here in 1988, must be the free beer at the end of the tour (if you are over 18). On the way, you will learn the story of Holland's most famous brewery, walk through the gleaming, white-tiled brewhouse with its huge copper stills, and visit the stables. The dray horses here are still to be seen carting beer, but only for publicity purposes. ◈ *Stadhouderskade 78 • Map D6 • 020 523 9666 • www.heinekenexperience.com • Open 10am–6pm Tue–Sun • Admission charge*

10 Albert Cuypmarkt

Shabby but vibrant, De Pijp is a district where a wide mix of immigrants, artists, students and young couples create a heady atmosphere. Albert Cuypmarkt, which has been trading since 1904, is its bustling hub. The street it occupies, once a canal, was named after Dutch landscape painter Albert Cuyp. With around 350 stalls, backed by all manner of shops and ethnic restaurants, it's an unmissable experience. Typically Dutch food stalls – cheese, fish, waffles – jostle merrily with clothes, fabrics, shoes and bags, all selling at rock-bottom prices. ◈ *Albert Cuypstraat • Map D6 • Open 9:30am–5pm Mon–Sat*

Smoked fish in Albert Cuypmarkt

Exploring the Eastern Canal Ring

Morning

On a fine stretch of the **Amstel River**, dainty Magere Brug makes a good spot to begin. Walking north, follow the river's curve, pausing at Amstel 104 and its equally crooked neighbours. Reaching **Munttoren**, wander along the **Bloemenmarkt**, then head down Reguliersbreestraat, where you can check your email at easyEverything (No. 22) before checking out the incredible **Tuschinski Theatre** a little further along the street.

Chic Utrechtsestraat, with its appealing selection of restaurants, cafés, delicatessens, boutiques and galleries, is perfect for both shopping and lunch. The best Indonesian *rijsttafel* in town is served at Tujuh Maret *(see p61)*.

Afternoon

From Utrechtsestraat cross to Amstelveld, where the wooden Amstelkerk lends a countrified air, and Reguliersgracht *(see p8)* intersects picturesquely with Prinsengracht. Make your way along Prinsengracht, cross Vijzelstraat, and dive into Weteringbuurt. On the other side of Prinsengracht, admire elegant Deutzenhofje (Nos 855–99), erected in 1695 for destitute women.

From here, it's only a short walk to the **Museum Van Loon** *(see pp30–31)*, or a little further to **Museum Willet-Holthuysen** *(see p107)*, after which you can wind down with a drink in jolly Rembrandtplein. Best cafés are Schiller *(see p113)* and De Kroon *(see p50)*.

Check out new photography museum Foam at Keizersgracht 609.

Left **April** Right **Soho**

🔟 Bars

1 April
A large, modern, comfortable gay bar that's great for reading a newspaper in the day or meeting up for drinks pre-clubbing. Unusual feature: the circular back bar revolves when it gets busy. 🅂 *Reguliersdwarsstraat 37 • Map M6*

2 Chocolate Bar
This trendy lounge bar-restaurant is a relatively new adddition to the Pijp area. 🅂 *Eerste van der Helststraat 62 • Map D6*

3 De Duivel
Cypress Hill and The Roots have joined the boisterous baggy brigade at Amsterdam's small but legendary hip hop bar. These days, the hip hop is melted down with anything from funk to disco. 🅂 *Reguliersdwarsstraat 87 • Map N6*

4 De Huyschkaemer
A corner-located, split-level designer bar-restaurant popular with a young arty crowd. Food is delicious and staff friendly. 🅂 *Utrechtsestraat 137 • Map E5 • 020 627 0575 • €€*

5 MME Jeanette
Knock back the cocktails while a DJ spins chillout music and upbeat house at this lounge bar-cum-restaurant serving international cuisine. 🅂 *Eerste van der Helststraat 42 • Map D6 • 020 673 3332 • €€*

6 Kingfisher
With its modern take on the brown bar style, this large bar is one of the best watering-holes in the Pijp. Imaginative world cuisine. 🅂 *Ferdinand Bolstraat 24 • Map D6 • 020 671 2395 • €*

7 Lellebel
Amsterdam's infamous – and only – dragshow bar, the complete antithesis of the testosterone-fuelled Rembrandt-plein nearby. At first glance it's unremarkable, but when Shirley Bassey is turned up on the soundsystem, the bar staff perform quite some routine. 🅂 *Utrechtsestraat 4 • Map P6*

8 Mulligans
If you're tired of the Rembrandtplein, pop round the corner to this authentic Irish bar for some good *craic*. 🅂 *Amstel 100 • Map P6*

9 Onder de Ooievaar
More of a wintertime bar, "Under the Stork" is warm, wooden and spacious. 🅂 *Utrechtse straat 119 • Map E5*

10 Soho
The "English pub formula" worked so well that Soho has become the biggest pint- and punter-puller on Amsterdam's trendy gay street. 🅂 *Reguliersdwarsstraat 36 • Map M6*

Price Categories

For a three course meal for one with half a bottle of wine (or equivalent meal), taxes and extra charges.

€	under €20
€€	€20–€30
€€€	€30–€45
€€€€	€45–€60
€€€€€	over €60

ushi

🔟 Restaurants

1 Eufraat
The décor leaves a little to be desired, but the fresh food at his Assyrian café makes it perpetually popular. A favourite haunt of revered (and feared) Amsterdam food critic Johannes an Dam. ◈ *Eerste van der Helstraat 2 • Map D6 • 020 672 0579 • €*

2 The Golden Temple
Vegetarian restaurant run by American Sikhs offering a range of Indian, Middle Eastern and Mexican food with a home-cooked feel. ◈ *Utrechtsestraat 26 • Map E5 • 020 626 8650 • €*

3 Inez IPSC
A discreet door leads up to his trendy establishment for hose with adventurous taste buds and fat wallets. ◈ *Amstel 2 • Map N5 • 020 639 2899 • €€€€*

4 Kitsch
Aficianados of kitsch will love he style of this perfectly pink restaurant. Ask for the corner mattress when booking, or a able with its own water fountain. ◈ *Utrechtse-straat 42 • Map E5 • 020 625 9251 • €€€*

5 Moko
Indulge your hedonistic tenden-cies at this fabulous bar-restaurant – at a price, of course. ◈ *Amstelveld 12 • Map E5 • 020 626 1199 • €€€*

6 Rose's Cantina
This Mexican cantina has Tex-Mex down to a tee – the food is varied and delicious, and the margaritas are served in pitchers! ◈ *Reguliersdwarsstraat 38 • Map M6 • 020 625 9797 • €€*

7 SSK
Hanneke cooks fresh produce she's bought from the markets that day, and serves you from her open kitchen. One of the city's best kept secrets. ◈ *Falckstraat 3 • Map E5 • 020 330 1128 • €€*

8 Utrechtsedwarfstafel
Pick a number of courses, choose a range from simple to gastronomic, and leave the rest to the wine connoisseur and cook duo who run this unusual eaterie. ◈ *Utrechtsedwarsstraat 107-109 • Map E5 • 020 625 4189 • €€€€*

9 Zuidlande
Eight is the magic number. If you reserve this table, you'll be wined and dined through at least 10 imaginative courses – or opt for a less decadent four-course menu. ◈ *Utrechtse-dwarsstraat 141 • Map E5 • 020 620 7393 • €€€€*

10 Zushi
Hyper-modern and hyped-up, this is the place to be if you like your sushi with a zing. ◈ *Amstel 20 • Map P6 • 020 330 6882 • €€*

Left **Tóth-Ikonen** Right **Galerie Elisabeth den Beiman de Haas**

🔟 Antique Shops

1 Aalderink
Aalderink is the oldest and most reputable dealer of Asian Art and Ethnographics in the Netherlands, specializing in fine Japanese *netsuke* and *okimono*. ◈ *Spiegelgracht 15 • Map D5*

2 Aronson Antiquairs
David Aronson opened this prestigious gallery around 1900; now it is run by his great- and great-great-grandsons. Early Delftware, continental 17th- and 18th-century furniture, plus Chinese *famille verte* and *famille rose* porcelain – much of it rare. ◈ *Nieuwe Spiegelstraat 39 • Map D5*

3 E H Ariëns Kappers / C P J van der Peet BV
This husband and wife team offers a huge range of mid 16th- to mid-20th-century prints, including a remarkable selection of Japanese woodblock prints. ◈ *Nieuwe Spiegelstraat 32 • Map D5*

4 Galerie Elisabeth den Bieman de Haas
Purveyors of fine contemporary art. ◈ *Nieuwe Spiegelstraat 44 • Map D5*

5 Frans Leidelmeijer
A testament to taste, this decorative arts shop was featured in an issue of *Wallpaper** not so long ago. ◈ *Nieuwe Spiegelstraat 58 • Map D5*

6 Eduard Kramer
Decorative Dutch tiles, Blue Delftware, antique books, prints, pewter, candlesticks and lamps. ◈ *Nieuwe Spiegelstraat 64 • Map D5*

7 Thom & Lenny Nelis
A fascinating collection of medical instruments dating from the early 18th to the early 20th century. Dissection kits, dental tools, apothecary accoutrements and much more! ◈ *Keizersgracht 54 • Map M6*

8 Tóth-Ikonen
The only icon specialist in the Spiegelkwartier, and the oldest in Amsterdam. Behold a dazzling array of 16th- to 19th-century Russian icons – including a large collection of brass travelling icons ◈ *Nieuwe Spiegelstraat 68 • Map D5*

9 Marjan Sterk
An exquisite selection of antique, Art Deco and Art Nouveau jewellery, plus 18th- and 19th-century Dutch silver. ◈ *Nieuwe Spiegelstraat 63 • Map D5*

10 Van Dreven Antiquair
Alive with the sound of ticking, this shop proffers an eclectic selection of clocks from the early 17th century to the 1930s plus a treasured collection of music boxes. ◈ *Nieuwe Spiegelstraat 38 • Map D5*

ft **Schiller Hotel** Right **Bloemenmarkt**

10 Best of the Rest

1 Backstage
A bizarre café-cum-crochet
tore run by Gary, one half of the
egendary "Christmas Twins", a
S cabaret duo. Pop in here for
ome "foam in rome" (cappucino),
spontaneous horoscope reading
y Gary, or simply for cake and
ossip. ◎ *Utrechtsedwarsstraat 67 •*
ap E5

2 Bloemenmarkt
The legendary floating
ower market *(see p108)*.

3 Concerto
Simply the best record store
town; new and secondhand. ◎
trechtsestraat 52–60 • Map E5

4 Soup en Zo
This one-stop modern soup
tchen is just a short walk from
e Rijksmuseum. Great for take-
ways, but some seats are
vailable. Over half the soups are
egetarian. ◎ *Nieuwe Spiegelstraat 54*
Map D5

5 Hemp Hotel
Little escapes being
empified at this
mall, family-run
otel – from the
emp futons to the
esh hemp muffins
erved at breakfast,
nd the hemp beer
erved in the late-
pening Hemple
emple Nightbar. ◎
ederiksplein 15 • Map
5 • 020 625 4425

6 Heineken Experience
If you're here for the beer,
this self-guided tour of the original
Heineken brewery is a must.
Entrance includes three glasses
of the famous brew *(see p109)*.

7 Magere Brug
The city's best-known bridge
– worth a wander for perfect
photo opportunites, the stunning
views, or simply to watch the
drawbridge in action. Romantic at
night when it's all lit up *(see p11)*.

8 The Otherside
For a perfectly pink joint,
head to the city's only gay
coffeeshop – a bright, modern,
friendly place. ◎ *Reguliersdwarsstraat*
6 • Map M6

9 Schiller Hotel
The bar and restaurant are a
gorgeous Art Nouveau escape
from touristic Rembrandtplein.
Owned for the best part of the
last century by painter Frits
Schiller, it was a regular meeting
place for artists, and still has
something of that atmosphere.
Schiller's paintings
are displayed
throughout the
premises *(see p146)*.

10 Village Bagels
Delicious bagels
and fresh juices are
served at this New
York-style bagel
shop. ◎ *Vijzelstraat 137*
• Map D5

Waterlooplein Ⓜ

Around Town – Eastern Canal Ring

113

Left **Concertgebouw** Right **Café Vertigo, Nederlands Filmmuseum**

Museum Quarter

UNTIL THE LATE 19TH CENTURY, *the Museum Quarter lay outside the ci* *limits, a region of small farms and market gardens. Then the city counc* *designated it an area of art and culture, and plans were conceived for the* *first of Amsterdam's celebrated cultural institutions. With its great museums* *of art, an internationally renowned concert hall, the city's largest park and* *clutch of exclusive shopping streets, the Museum Quarter is today one of* *Amsterdam's most impressive areas.*

🔟 Sights

1. **Rijksmuseum**
2. **Van Gogh Museum**
3. **Stedelijk Museum**
4. **Concertgebouw**
5. **Vondelpark**
6. **Coster Diamonds**
7. **Museumplein**
8. **Nederlands Filmmuseum**
9. **Hollandse Manege**
10. **P C Hooftstraat**

Rijksmuseum

Rijksmuseum

1 Established by King Louis Napoleon in 1808 along the lines of the Paris Louvre, the Rijksmuseum collection has grown in the intervening years to nearly seven million works of art. It has moved twice since its beginnings in the Royal Palace on the Dam. Since 1885 it has been housed in P J H Cuypers' ornate Neo-Gothic building *(see pp12–15)*.

Van Gogh Museum

2 The uncompromisingly modern building by De Stijl architect Gerrit Rietveld was specially designed to display the nation's collection of this disturbed yet brilliant artist's work *(see pp16–19)*.

Stedelijk Museum

3 Devoted to modern art from the mid-19th century to the present day, this invigorating museum is undergoing a total renovation. Until it reopens in 2005, works from the collection will remain on display at various venues in Amsterdam. ✎ *Paulus Potterstraat 13 • Map C6 • 020 573 2911 • www.stedelijk.nl*

Concertgebouw

4 One of the world's great concert halls, the Concertgebouw was built in 1888, designed by A L Van Gendt in Neo-Dutch Renaissance style with a colonnaded Neo-Classical façade. In the 1980s, the building was discovered to be in danger of collapse. In time for the centenary of both the concert hall and its world-famous orchestra, new foundations were laid, and the building was restored and enlarged. Amazingly, all this took place without its having to close. ✎ *Concertgebouwplein 2–6 • Map C6 • 020 671 8345 • www.concertgebouw.nl • Box office open 10am–7pm daily*

Vondelpark

5 Founded in 1864 by a group of philanthropic citizens, this congenial park was later named after the 17th-century poet Joost van den Vondel. Landscaped on informal English lines in 1865 – and enlarged in 1877 – by father and son J D and L P Zocher, with wide green vistas, a profusion of trees and lakes, a rose garden and a bandstand, it became a mecca for hippies in the late 1960s and 1970s. It is still a lively place on summer Sundays, when people flock to hear concerts and plays in the open-air theatre, glimpse the occasional juggler or fire-eater, jog, rollerblade or play football. There are many different species of plants, trees and wildlife. A distinctive landmark, looking a little like a neat boater turned upside-down, is the round Blauwe Theehuis (teahouse), built by H A J Baanders in 1936 in the New Functionalist style. ✎ *Stadhouderskade • Map A6*

Bandstand in Vondelpark

Coster Diamonds

Founded in 1840 and now occupying three grand villas, Coster is one of a handful of diamond workshops offering guided tours. About 30 minutes in length, they give you the opportunity to observe stone graders, cutters and polishers at work. In 1852, the *Koh-i-Noor* (mountain of light) diamond was re-polished here for the British Crown Jewels, and a replica of the crown that contains it – incorporating a copy of the fabulous blue-white stone – is displayed in the entrance hall. If your budget will allow it, there are also diamonds and jewellery for sale over the counter. ⊗ *Paulus Potterstraat 2–8 • Map C5 • 020 305 5555 • www.costerdiamonds.com • Open 9am–5pm daily • Free*

Coster Diamonds

Museumplein

The city's largest square was first landscaped in 1872, but it was ruined in 1953 when a hair-raising stretch of road – which locals nicknamed "the shortest motorway in Europe" – was built across it. Completely redesigned between 1990 and 1996, it is now a great swathe of green, still more functional than beautiful but giving an uninterrupted view from the Rijksmuseum to the Concertgebouw. It has children's play areas and a pond that is frozen over to form an ice-rink in winter. Various events are staged here – from circuses to political demonstrations – and it is the setting for *Hel van Vuur* (Hell of Fire), a monument to all gypsies persecuted by the Nazis, as well as the Ravensbrück Memorial *(see p49)*. The district is one of the wealthiest in Amsterdam, with broad streets lined by grand houses. ⊗ *Map C6*

Nederlands Filmmuseum

"Museum" is a slight misnomer for this institution, as the Nederlands Filmmuseum no longer has an exhibition. What it does have is an archive of more than 30,000 films, ranging from classic to art-house, a selection of which is screened here throughout the year. The entire collection is housed in a glorious 19th-century pavilion at the edge of the Vondelpark. The building, designed by architects P J Hamer and his son W Hamer, opened in 1881 as a fashionable teahouse. It has since undergone two major renovations, in 1947 and 1991. ⊗ *Vondelpark 3 • Map B5 • Box Office: 020 589 1400. www.filmmuseum.nl • Information Centre: Vondelstraat 69–71. 020 589 1435 • Open 10am–5pm Tue–Fri, 11am–5pm Sat; closed mid-Jul to mid-Aug*

Hollandse Manege

Hollandse Manege

9 Magnificent and quite unexpected, concealed behind an unexceptional façade, A L van Gendt's Hollandse Manege is a vast Neo-Classical indoor riding school, built in 1881. (It was commissioned to replace the original Dutch Riding School building, which was situated on Leidsegracht.) Based on the Spanish Riding School in Vienna, it sports elegant plasterwork, sculpted horses' heads, and a stunning open ironwork roof rising high above the sand arena. The school was threatened with demolition in the 1980s, but public outcry saved it. If there is a lesson in progress, you can stay and watch. There is also a café. ⊗ *Vondelstraat 140 • Map B5 • 020 618 0942 • Open 10am–midnight Tue–Fri, 10am–6pm Sat & Sun, 2pm–midnight Mon • Free*

P C Hooftstraat

10 This elegant shopping street is to Amsterdam what Bond Street is to London. All the names in international fashion are here – Tommy Hilfiger, Hugo Boss, DKNY, Gucci, Mulberry, Emporio Armani – although well-heeled locals tend to favour friendlier Cornelis Schuystraat nearby. ⊗ *Map C5*

A Day in the Museum Quarter

Morning

Depending on your taste in art, start the day either in the **Rijksmuseum** *(see pp12–15)* or the **Van Gogh Museum** *(see pp16–19)*. If you choose the former, be selective, and do bear in mind that from late 2003, the main building will be closed for restoration, *(see p12)*. Whichever museum you visit, you should aim to spend the whole morning there. The Van Gogh Museum has a useful ground floor café, and you can end your visit with a browse in the museum shop next to the main entrance.

Next, cross **Museumplein** to the **Concertgebouw** *(see p115)* and pop in for a look. Make your way to Art Deco Brasserie van Baerle (Van Baerlestraat 158) for lunch. It has a lovely shady garden and is popular, so it's worth booking a table.

Afternoon

Head back to Paulus Potterstraat and **Coster Diamonds**, where you could take one of the half-hour tours. Afterwards, walk along Hobbemastraat until you reach the elegant shops of **P C Hooftstraat**. Turn left and window-shop your way along the street.

If your feet are up to it, spend an hour or so strolling around the Vondelpark, finishing either at the Blauwe Theehuis *(see p50)* or the **Nederlands Filmmuseum's** Café Vertigo, which has a lovely terrace overlooking the park. You could end with a visit to the **Hollandse Manege**, which opens till midnight on weekdays.

Bakkerswinkel van Nineties

Around Town – Museum Quarter

Food and Drink

1 Bakkerswinkel van Nineties
This bakery with seats inside is an ideal spot for breakfast, lunch or high tea – but beware, it can get crowded. ◎ *Roelof Hartstraat 68*

2 Cadans
Chef Pjotr Rentinck serves up French cuisine in this classy new establishment. ◎ *Roelof Hartstraat 6–8 • 020 676 5201 • €€€€*

3 Brasserie van Baerle
This polished contemporary brasserie is popular with Dutch celebs for its well-reputed wine list, imaginative French cuisine, languishing lunches and hedonistic Sunday brunches. ◎ *Van Baerlestraat 158 • Map C6 • 020 679 1532 • €€€*

4 CoBrA Café
Designer café on Museumplein created as an ode to the members of the CoBrA art movement. Wine and dine in the restaurant, or go Japanese at the stylish sushi bar. ◎ *Hobbemastraat 18 • Map C6 • 020 470 0111 • €€*

5 Café Ebeling
A relaxed, spacious bar popular with a younger, trendier crowd. ◎ *Overtoom 52 • Map C5*

6 Le Garage
The famous and beautiful of Amsterdam fill their tummies and empty their wallets here. The food is a delicate fusion of French with international cuisine. ◎ *Ruysdaelstraat 54–56 • Map C6 • 020 679 7176 • €€€*

7 De Groene Gewoonte
If you like your food pure, head for this small, organic restaurant on a rather ordinary street. ◎ *Tweede Helmersstraat 3 • Map J6 • 020 689 8952 • €*

8 De Orient
A family-run Indonesian restaurant serving good-value, creative meals with plenty to tempt the vegetarian pallet. ◎ *Van Baerlestraat 21 • Map C6 • 020 673 4958 • €€*

9 Café Toussaint
This charming café-bar has an open kitchen from which delicious lunches and dinners are served. Ideal for relaxed, sunny days or warm, intimate evenings ◎ *Bosboom Toussaintstraat 26 • Map J6 • 020 685 0737 • €*

10 Wildschut
Take in the surrounding Amsterdam School architectural styles from the terrace of this grand café famous for its Art Deco interior. ◎ *Roelof Hartplein 1–3 • 020 676 8220 • €€*

Left **Filmmuseum terrace** Right **Concertgebouw**

10 Best of the Rest

1 Altena Zeebanket Van
One of the best places in town to try the traditional Dutch custom of slipping a raw herring down your gullet. The less brave can settle for a salmon sandwich. ◈ *Stadhouderskade 41 • Map D5*

2 Het Blauwe Theehuis
This teahouse in the Vondelpark is one of the city's best-kept secrets, despite its central location. ◈ *Vondelpark • Map B6*

3 Broekmans & Van Poppel
Founded in 1914, this store has one of the largest collections of sheet music in the world. ◈ *Van Baerlestraat 92–94 • Map C6*

4 Concertgebouw
Every Wednesday at 12:30pm (except in summer) there are free lunchtime concerts here. Atmosphere informal, quality unsurpassed; queue early *(see p115)*.

5 Filmmuseum
Don't miss the live musical performances to silent classics, or the open-air screenings from the historic building's balcony in summer *(see p116)*.

6 Friday Night Skate
Join this huge group of skaters for a free, two-hour, 15 km (9 mile) tour of the city. Anyone who is reasonably proficient can join in. Gather from 8pm. ◈ *Vondelpark (Roemer Visscherstraat entrance) • Map C5*

7 Hollandse Manege
One of the more unusual places to stop for a drink in town. The upstairs café of this stables overlooks the sand arena below as classes are being held *(see p117)*.

8 De Peperwortel
Just two minutes from the Filmmuseum, this charming *traiteur* is ideally placed for picnicking in the park. Delicious quiches, pasta, salads and soup, with vegetarians well catered for. Plus a choice selection of wine. ◈ *Overtoom 140 • Map B5*

9 Vondelpark Openluchttheater
Catch a bit of drama, flamenco, puppetry or pop in the Vondelpark's open-air theatre. ◈ *Vondelpark • Map B6 • end May–end Aug: Wed–Sun*

10 Zuiderbad
This recently restored Art Nouveau swimming pool, dating from 1911, is the city's most stylish place to bathe. Regular evening concerts are held here. ◈ *Hobbemastraat 26 • Map D6*

For more information on the Friday Night Skate, visit www.fridaynightskate.com

Left **Koninklijk Theater Carré** Right **Werf't Kromhout Museum**

Plantage

VISITORS FLOCK TO AMSTERDAM'S EXCELLENT ZOO, *but the rest of this distinguished residential district, with its elegant villas and broad, tree-lined streets, is often overlooked. Most of the villas appeared in the 19th century, many of them occupied by Jews who had prospered in the diamond industry, and the neighbourhood's strong Jewish tradition is reflected in its numerous memorials. Plantage means plantation: this was a rural area until the final extension of the Grachtengordel in 1638. Despite its tranquillity, there is no shortage of places to visit and sights to see.*

🔟 Sights

1. Nederlands Scheepvaart Museum
2. Artis
3. Entrepotdok
4. Werf't Kromhout Museum
5. Verzetsmuseum
6. Hortus Botanicus
7. De Burcht
8. Hollandse Schouwburg
9. Koninklijk Theater Carré
10. Amstelhof

Entrepotdok

1 Nederlands Scheepvaart Museum

For anyone who loves ships, the maritime museum is a must. Where sails, ropes, guns and munitions were once stored is now an Aladdin's Cave of nautical treasures. Don't miss the Orrery of Jan Van den Dam in Room 9, the fabulous Royal Barge on the ground floor and the East Indiaman Amsterdam, moored outside (see pp41 and 68). ✎ Kattenburgerplein 1 • Map G3 • 020 523 2222 • www.scheepvaart-museum.nl • Open 10am–5pm Tue–Sun & public hols; also open 10am–5pm Mon during school holidays • Admission charge

2 Artis

If you want to give human culture a break, the zoological garden makes a terrific contrast. About 900 species are kept in reasonably naturalistic surroundings, including a recently created African landscape. Watch the Japanese monkeys grooming one another, the reptiles slithering in their steamy jungle, or the polar bears lazing with menacing unconcern. There are plenty of places where you can shelter from the rain, including the Planetarium, Geological and Zoological museums, and the Aquarium, home to more than 2,000 mesmerizing fish. ✎ Plantage Kerklaan 38–40 • Map G4 • 020 523 3400 • www.artis.nl • Open summer: 9am–6pm daily; winter: 9am–5pm daily • Guided tour 11am Sun • Admission charge

3 Entrepotdok

The flat brick façades of these typical 19th-century warehouses, punctuated by shuttered, arched windows, seem to stretch endlessly along the dockside. When owned by the Dutch East India Company (VOC), they were declared part of a free port, and no duties were levied here on cargoes in transit. Now they have been converted into offices and apartments, served by pleasant cafés and restaurants, whose tables line the canal in summer. ✎ Map G4

4 Werf 't Kromhout Museum

In the 18th century, the Eastern docklands were packed with shipyards. Today this recently restored working yard is one of the few remaining. It has survived by moving with the times – concentrating on restoration when shipbuilding declined, producing the diesel engine that powered most inland waterways craft, and doubling as a museum. Its displays include tools, machinery, steam engines, photographs and an exhibition on 300 years of shipbuilding in the area. ✎ Hoogte Kadijk 147 • Map G4 • 020 627 6777 • Open 10am–3pm Tue • Groups by appointment • Admission charge

Artis Planetarium

123

The Dutch East India Company (VOC)

Amsterdam's wealth in the 17th century was in no small measure due to the success of the VOC. Founded in 1602, it had a trading monopoly east of the Cape of Good Hope. Its legendary fleet of "East Indiamen" *(see p68)* carried much of Europe's spice imports until it folded in 1791.

Verzetsmuseum

5 Following the development of the Dutch Resistance movement from the German invasion in May 1940 to the liberation in May 1945, this exhibition shows how the Dutch people courageously faced the occupation. Its fascinating and evocative displays relate private stories of individual heroism and place them in their historical context. Among the memorabilia are forged identity papers, old photographs, underground newspapers and deadly weapons. ✪ *Plantage Kerklaan 61 • Map G4 • 020 620 2535 • www.verzetsmuseum.org • Open 10am–5pm Tue–Fri, noon–5pm Sat & Sun • Admission charge*

Hortus Botanicus

6 About 8,000 different species of plants, flowers and trees, an ornamental pond, rock and herb

Hortus Botanicus

De Burcht

gardens, and numerous glasshouses are crammed into this small, wedge-shaped botanical garden. Most of the exotic plants were collected by the VOC in the 17th and 18th centuries. Highlights are a 300-year old Cycad palm, the three-climates glasshouse and a coffee plant, Europe's first, smuggled out of Ethiopia in 1706. ✪ *Plantage Middenlaan 2A • Map R5 • 020 625 9021 • www.dehortus.nl • Open Apr–Oct: 9am–5pm Mon–Fri, 11am–5pm Sat, Sun & public hols; Nov–Mar: 9am–4pm Mon–Fri, 11am–4pm Sat, Sun & public hols • Admission charge*

De Burcht (Vakbondsmuseum)

7 Nicknamed "the castle" because of its crenellated façade, this is the oldest Trades Union building in the Netherlands, built in 1900 by H P Berlage of Beurs fame *(see p84)* for the General Dutch Diamond Workers' Union (ANDB). Go inside for the stunning tiled entrance hall and staircase, and murals by Richard Roland Holst of the Amsterdam School. ✪ *Henri Polaklaan 9 • Map F4 • 020 624 1166 • www.deburcht-vakbondsmuseum.nl • Open 11am–5pm Tue–Fri, 1–5pm Sun • Admission charge*

Hollandse Schouwburg

8 During the Nazi occupation, this former theatre was used as an assembly-point for between 60,000 and 80,000 Jews. Behind an intact façade, a garden has been created around a basalt monument on the site of the auditorium. The names of 6,700 Dutch Jews are engraved in a memorial hall to the 104,000 who were exterminated. There is an exhibition upstairs. ◉ *Plantage Middenlaan 24 • Map F4 • 020 626 9945 • Open 11am–4pm daily • Free*

Koninklijk Theater Carré

9 It is hard to believe that the magnificent Carré Theatre, superbly set beside the Amstel, was built at break-neck speed in 1887 to house Oscar Carré's circus. A copy of his other circus in Cologne, it has a fine Neo-Renaissance frontage, some splendid ironwork, and is decorated appropriately with the heads of clowns and dancers. Today, it hosts pop concerts, dance shows, lavish musicals, and even the occasional circus. ◉ *Amstel 115–25 • Map F5 • 0900 252 255 • www.theatercarre.nl • Box office open 9am–9pm daily • Guided tours 3pm Wed & Sat*

Amstelhof

10 When this sober *hofje* was completed in 1683, it was the widest building in Amsterdam. It was part of the final phase of work on the Grachtengordel *(see p11)*, when the three canals were extended beyond the Amstel and given the prefix "Nieuwe". The city had difficulty in selling off the land, and was eventually forced to let charities have it at bargain prices. A project is under way to convert it into an outpost of the Hermitage Museum in St Petersburg. ◉ *Amstel 51 • Map E4*

A Day in the Plantage

Morning

Start your day among the cannons, models, figureheads, maps and instruments of the **Nederlands Scheepvaart Museum** *(see p123)*, then revive yourself at the pleasant ground-floor café. If you secretly hanker after a ship-in-a-bottle, a cutlass paper knife or other objects with a nautical theme, visit the museum shop before you leave. Outside, take a look around the Amsterdam, the full-size replica of an 18th-century East Indiaman, manned by actors.

If it is a Tuesday and you haven't yet had your fill of boats, take a short detour to the **Werf 't Kromhout Museum** *(see p123)* to see some shipbuilding in progress or, at the very least, the exhibition about it. Lunch at one of the cafés in **Entrepotdok** – perhaps Entredok at No. 64.

Afternoon

After lunch, you could make your way to Plantage Kerklaan and the **Verzetsmuseum** *(see facing page)*. A visit here is definitely worthwhile, if harrowing. Afterwards, blow the cobwebs away by spending an hour or two at **Artis** *(see p123)*. For a few euros, the excellent zoo plan gives you feeding times, as well as pinpointing the two museums and the revamped Aquarium. Head back towards the main entrance, where there is a café, and a shop selling goods with a wildlife theme. If there is time, you could finish your explorations with a quick dash around the solar system at the Planetarium.

Around Town – Plantage

Left **De Rieker Windmill, Amstelpark** Right **Ouderkerk aan de Amstel**

Further Afield

CENTRAL AMSTERDAM HAS MORE THAN ENOUGH *to keep any visitor occupied, but if time permits, it's certainly worth taking the trouble to explore the outskirts, where a diverse selection of sights is on offer. Football fans will want to make a beeline for the city's stunning new stadium, Amsterdam ArenA, home of legendary soccer club Ajax. There are fascinating exhibits on view at the Cobra Museum, the Tropenmuseum, NEMO and the Aviodome. If you are interested in architecture, make sure that you see the innovative 1920s buildings of the De Dageraad housing estate. If it's peace and quiet you want, there are several choices, including the small, historic town of Ouderkerk aan de Amstel – older than Amsterdam itself – and the wide open spaces of Amsterdamse Bos. The city's excellent transport system makes all these sights easily accessible, and some of them are not far from the centre – or from each other.*

 Sights

1. Tropenmuseum
2. De Dageraad Housing
3. Amstelpark
4. Ajax Museum
5. Ouderkerk aan de Amstel
6. Amsterdamse Bos
7. Cobra Museum
8. Java Eiland and KNSM Eiland
9. NEMO
10. Aviodome

De Dageraad Housing

openmuseum

1 Tropenmuseum

Take a trip around the world without leaving this imposing 1920s building, originally conceived to celebrate Dutch colonialism but now redeployed to educate visitors about the developing world. Reconstructions whether of an Arabian bazaar, an African village or an Indian slum – are vividly brought to life with the help of soundtracks and even smells. The separate Kinder-museum is strictly for 6–12-year-olds (no admission to an adult unless accompanied by a child), by appointment, with guided tours in Dutch. ◎ *Linnaeusstraat 2 • Tram 9, 10, 14; bus 22 • Tropenmuseum: 020 568 8215. Kindermuseum: 020 568 8233 • www.tropenmuseum.nl • Open 10am–5pm daily • Admission charge*

2 De Dageraad Housing

A housing estate seems an unlikely tourist attraction, but the complex built for the De Dageraad (Dawn) housing association from 1918–23 is well worth a visit – specially for anyone interested in the Amsterdam School of architecture, of which this is a prime example. Piet Kramer and Michel de Klerk designed sculptural buildings of great originality, with tiled roofs that undulate in waves, and brick walls that billow and curve to produce an effect of horizontal movement. The project was part of an initiative to provide better housing for poorer families, in the wake of the revolutionary Housing Act of 1901. ◎ *Pieter Lodewijk Takstraat • Tram 4,12,25*

3 Amstelpark

This welcome green space to the south of the city has a rose garden, a maze and an art gallery for adults, as well as pony rides, farm animals and a miniature steam train for children. Best of all, at the southernmost tip of the park, is the well-preserved De Rieker windmill. Built in 1636, it was a favourite of Rembrandt, whose statue stands nearby. Now a private home, its sails are unfurled on National Windmill Day (second Sat in May). ◎ *Europaboulevard • Open dawn–dusk*

4 Ajax Museum

Football fans will want to pay their respects to the brilliant Ajax club at their impressive new stadium, Amsterdam ArenA. If you can't see them play, at least visit the interactive museum, which brings the club and its greatest moments to life, and tour the state-of-the-art 50,000-seat stadium, including the pitch and players' benches. There are usually six tours a day in summer, four in winter, except on event days; phone ahead for times. ◎ *Arena Boulevard 1 • Metro to Strandvliet or Bijlmer; train to Bijlmer • 020 311 1333 • www.amsterdamarena.nl • Open 9am–6pm daily • Admission charge*

Ajax Museum

5 Ouderkerk aan de Amstel

There was no church in town until 1330 (see p28), so people came instead to this picturesque riverside village to worship at the 11th-century Oude Kerk that stood here until it was destroyed by a storm in 1674. Convivial waterside cafés and restaurants are the chief lure these days, but you can also walk in the wooded garden of an 18th-century house, Wester Amstel, and visit an unexpected site: the Beth Haim Jewish cemetery. Amsterdam's Jews have been buried here since 1615, when they were forbidden burial in the city. 🏵 Metro or train to Bijlmer, then bus 174, 175

6 Amsterdamse Bos

Just a short bus, old-fashioned tram (see p68) or bike ride away, this attractive woodland park makes a wonderful contrast to the city. Laid out on reclaimed land in the 1930s with the dual purpose of creating jobs for the unemployed and providing more recreation space, the park has woods and meadows, lakes and nature reserves. There is plenty to do: hire bicycles, go boating, eat pancakes, visit the bison and the goats and the Bos Museum, which describes the park and how it was built. 🏵 Amstelveenseweg • Bus 170, 171, 172 • Open permanently

City of Cyclists

Cycling comes as naturally to Amsterdammers as walking, royal family included. There are about 600,000 bikes in the city – almost one per person. Theft is endemic, so snazzy models are avoided. Look out for: the huge bike shed at Centraal Station; bikes being dredged up from canals; the eight-man "conference bike" and the heart-shaped "love bike".

Amsterdamse Bos

7 Cobra Museum

This museum of modern art in residential Amstelveen is dedicated in part to the influential Dutch movement conceived in 1948. Its founders, including Dutchman Karel Appel (see p47), amalgamated the names of their home cities – Copenhagen, Brussels and Amsterdam – to create its name: CoBrA. They wanted to promote art that was spontaneous and inclusive, and were inspired by the work of primitives, children and the mentally ill. Paintings in the permanent collection are shown in changing thematic displays, augmented by temporary exhibitions. The light, spare building, by Wim Quist, opened in 1995. 🏵 Sandbergplein 1–3, Amstelveen • Tram 5 to Binnenhof • 020 547 5050 • www.cobra-museum.nl • Open 11am–5pm Tue–Sun • Admission charge

8 Java Eiland and KNSM Eiland

These former docks, outposts of the Eastern Islands, have been the subject of intense development and renovation in the last decade, in response to the city's need for new housing. They are now considered trendy places to live, and designer home shops, boutiques, restaurants and cafés are springing up. They are most easily reached by the Javabrug footbridge from Oostelijke Handelskade. 🏵 Bus 32

NEMO

9 The most arresting feature of this interactive science and technology centre – the largest in the Netherlands – is the building itself. Designed by Renzo Piano, its harbour location (in the Eastern Islands) gave the impetus for a green copper structure resembling a vast ship. The great views from the top deck will certainly appeal, even if the hands-on games, experiments and demonstrations, designed to entertain and educate both children and adults, do not. ✪ *Oosterdok 2 • Bus 22, 32 • 0900 919 100 • www.e-nemo.nl • Open 10am–5pm Tue–Sun, also Mon during school holidays • Admission charge*

Aviodome

10 The Dutch national aviation museum is currently housed in a giant aluminium dome at Schiphol Airport, with more than 30 historic aircraft on show, as well as spacecraft and coin-operated flight simulators. The museum on this site is due to close, and at some point in 2003 it will reopen at Lelystad Airport as an interactive aviation theme park. Check the Aviodome website for details. ✪ *Westelijke Randweg 201, Schiphol Centrum • Train to Schiphol, then signposted • 020 406 8000 • www. aviodome.nl • Open Apr–Sep: 10am–5pm daily; Oct–Mar: 10am–5pm Tue–Fri, noon–5pm Sat & Sun • Admission charge*

Aviodome

A Day Out with the Kids

Morning

🕐 You don't have to take children to enjoy this suggested day out, but it will appeal to them if you do. It's wise to phone the Ajax Museum in advance, to check on its tour times.

Start by taking tram 9, 10 or 14, or bus 22 to the **Tropenmuseum** *(see p127)*, where you can take a whistlestop tour of the developing world. Afterwards, have an exotic lunch in the museum's lush café-restaurant, Ekeko, and don't forget the shop, with its range of ethnic gifts.

Afternoon

Walk along Linnaeusstraat, leaving Oosterpark on your right, and turn left along Domselaerstraat to find Muiderpoort Station. Catch one of the frequent *stoptreins* in the direction of Utrecht for the 9-minute ride to Bijlmer Station to visit the Amsterdam ArenA. The **Ajax Museum** *(see page 127)* and its guided tour of the stadium will fill your afternoon.

If you want to extend your trip into the evening, consider taking a short bus ride (Nos 174 or 175) from Bijlmer station to the picturesque village of **Ouderkerk aan de Amstel**, with its waterside cafés and restaurants.

If it's a Sunday between April and October, you may prefer to take a day trip to **Amsterdamse Bos** (and perhaps to the **Cobra Museum** at Amstelveen), using the Electrische Museumtramlijn to get you there and back.

Catch the Electrische Museumtramlijn at Haarlemmermeerstation (No.16 tram from Centraal Station).

STREETSMART

AMSTERDAM'S TOP 10

Left **Euro notes** Right **Umbrellas on a rainy day**

🔟 Planning Your Trip

1 Choosing an Area
Most tourist hotels are to be found in one of three areas: the historic centre, the Museum Quarter and the atmospheric *Grachtengordel* (Canal Ring) with its gabled canal houses. Many business-oriented hotels are located a little further afield in the *Nieuw Zuid* (New South).

2 What to Pack
Be prepared for all weathers, and bring an umbrella, a waterproof jacket and a sweater – even in summer. Comfortable walking shoes are essential. Amsterdammers' dress style is casual and often creative. Few places insist on formality – casinos are an exception – but you can dress up for concerts and smart hotels and restaurants.

3 Passports and Other Documents
You must have a valid passport to enter the Netherlands. Citizens of EU countries, the USA, Australia and New Zealand need no visa as long as the stay is for less than three months. Passports must be valid for at least three months beyond the end of your stay. Citizens of other countries should consult their Dutch embassy or consulate for information. It is advisable to take out travel and health insurance before travelling.

4 Customs
Apart from offensive weapons, plants and perishable foods, there are few limits on what EU nationals can import for personal use. Non-EU citizens can buy duty-free goods up to the current limit. Cats and dogs are allowed, provided they have a certificate of inoculation against rabies. Flower bulbs may be exported from the Netherlands; for the USA, an inoculation certificate is required. Bulbs are best mailed home; the dealer should carry out all of the necessary paperwork.

5 Currency
For security, bring a cash card or traveller's cheques. Make sure that your cash withdrawal card is accepted in the Netherlands – most are. Bring some euros to pay for immediate needs on arrival. There is no limit on how much currency you can bring in or take out of the country.

6 Driving
If you are planning to drive your own car, you must bring an EU or International Driver's Licence, valid insurance documents, proof of registration, road safety certificate and international identification disc. To hire a car, you must be 21 or over, with a valid driving licence and a credit card.

7 Electricity
The electricity supply in the Netherlands is 220 volts AC. British visitors should bring a two-pin adaptor for their three-pin plugs. Americans need to convert their equipment or buy a transformer, as Dutch wall sockets require a larger plug.

8 Time Difference
The Netherlands is on Central European Time, one hour ahead of GMT. Like the rest of the EU and the USA, it observes Daylight Saving Time, so it remains one hour ahead of the UK and six hours ahead of New York all year round.

9 Children's Needs
If you have very young children, it is best to carry them in baby slings; pushchairs are difficult to manoeuvre on the cobbled streets, and almost impossible to get on and off crowded trams and canal boats. Most places accept children, except for some expensive restaurants.

🔟 Public Holidays
Public holidays are as follows: New Year's Day (1 Jan); *Eerste Paasdag* (Easter Monday); *Koninginnedag* (30 Apr); *Bevrijdingsdag* (5 May); *Hemelvaartsdag* (Ascension Day); *Pinksteren* (Whitsun); *Eerste Kerstdag* (Christmas Day); *Tweede Kerstdag* (26 Dec).

Left Train at Centraal Station Right **Arriving by road**

10 Arriving in Amsterdam

1 Schiphol Airport
Amsterdam's airport is efficient, modern and easy to use, with an incredible range of facilities from golf to gambling. There is a single terminal, with one level for Arrivals and another level for Departures. Signs are colour-coded: yellow for transfer desks and gates, green for amenities. The Aviation Museum is, at present, housed in the nearby Aviodome *(see p129).* Flight information: 0900 7244 7465 • www.schiphol.nl

2 From Schiphol by Train
The best and cheapest method of getting from the airport to the city is by rail – access is by escalator from the shopping plaza where the tickets are on sale. Trains run direct to Centraal Station every 15 minutes from 6am to midnight, then every hour. Journey time is 20 minutes.

3 From Schiphol by Bus
Instead of the train, you can take the smart KLM Hotel Bus from outside the main exit. It stops at several city-centre hotels, leaving every 30 minutes between 6.30am and 3pm, and every hour between 3pm and 10pm. You can also take a taxi, but it's hardly worth the expense, considering the ease of public transport.

4 Arriving by Train
Whether you are travelling from Britain or from mainland Europe, you will arrive at Centraal Station. Its best feature is the Eerste Klas café *(see p51);* otherwise, it's crowded and prone to pickpockets and drug pushers, so head directly for the main entrance and Stationsplein. Here you will find the Amsterdam Tourist Board (VVV) and tram stop to the left, bus stops to the right. Eurostar enquiries and reservations: 0870 160 6600 • www.eurostar.com

5 Arriving by Road
Drive on the right. Speed limits are 100 kph (60 mph) or 120 kph (75 mph) on motorways, 80 kph (50 mph) outside cities, and 50 kph (30 mph) in built-up areas. From the A10 ring road, the S-routes (marked by blue signs) take you to the centre of Amsterdam. *(See Driving p132.)*

6 Parking
Driving in Amsterdam is best avoided. Stay in a hotel with secure parking, or leave your car in the park-and-ride facility at Amsterdam Arena, or in a covered public car park (indicated by a white P on a blue background). Muziektheater Parking: Waterlooplein. Map Q5 • Byzantium: Tesselschade-straat 19. Map C5 • Europarking: Marnixstraat 250. Map K6

7 Arriving by Ferry
From London, the boat-train service offered by Stena Sealink via Harwich and the Hook of Holland takes about 8 hours, and you will end your journey at Centraal Station. Otherwise, P&O ferries cross from Hull to Rotterdam, Dover to Zeebrugge or Felixstowe to Zeebrugge. P&O Stena Line: 08705 980 980 • www.posl.com

8 Bus and Coach
The cheapest option, but also the most tiring. From London's Victoria Coach Station, Eurolines coaches go via the Channel Tunnel or the ferry, taking between 9 and 12 hours to reach Amstel Station. Eurolines UK: 01582 404 511 • www.gobycoach.com

9 Car Hire
The major car hire companies have both airport and city-centre offices. For the best rates, try Dutch firms such as Diks or Kuperus. *(See Driving p132.)* Diks: 020 662 3366 • Kupurus: 020 668 3311 • Budget: 020 612 6066

10 Left Luggage
Both Schiphol Airport and Centraal Station have facilities for left luggage. At Schiphol there is a staffed counter, open from 7am–10.45pm, as well as lockers. At Centraal Station there are 24-hour lockers.

Left **Amsterdam Tourist Board** Right **Reference books in an Amsterdam library**

🔟 Sources of Information

1 Amsterdam Tourist Board

Still universally known by its old name, VVV, the Tourist Board has three offices in the city *(see below)*. At these you will find free maps, and leaflets on just about everything – including walks, canal tours, sights, exhibitions, transport and accommodation. Multi-lingual staff will give advice, change money, arrange excursions and – for a fee – book tickets and hotels. Here you can also buy the popular Amsterdam Pass and *Museumjaarkaart (see p136)*. 🖝 *0900 400 4040 • info@amsterdamtourist.nl*

2 Tourist Offices

There are three VVV offices in Amsterdam itself: at Centraal Station (Platform 2), at Stationsplein 10 (in front of the station), and at Leidseplein 1 (on the corner with Leidsestraat). There is another office at Schiphol Airport (Holland Tourist Information Arrivals 2).

3 NBT (Netherlands Board of Tourism)

You can pick up the NBT's own maps, information leaflets and brochures at any of its offices throughout the world. If you have a local branch, you should make a point of visiting it before you travel. 🖝 *www.holland.com*

4 Dutch Tourist Service

The friendly staff at this independent organization will make hotel reservations (even last-minute ones), book excursions and proffer helpful advice. 🖝 *Damrak 7 • Map P1 • 020 520 7000 • www.amsterdam-ts.nl • sales@amsterdam-ts.nl*

5 Websites

The Amsterdam Tourist Board has two official websites: www.amsterdamtourist.nl (in Dutch) and www.visit amsterdam.nl, which is linked to the NBT web-site, www.holland.com. The City of Amsterdam has its own website, www.amsterdam.nl. All of these have useful, up-to-date information on accommodation, events, exhibitions, shopping and travel (you can also book hotel rooms online). To find out what's on, visit www.amsterdam.uitlijn.nl The majority of the city's museums and attractions have their own websites.

6 Accommodation

To book hotels before you travel, contact the Amsterdam Reservation Center, a branch of the Amsterdam Tourist Board. 🖝 *PO Box 3901, NL–1001 AS Amsterdam • 0900 400 4040 • reservations @amsterdamtourist.nl*

7 Publications

The best listings magazine in Dutch is *Uitkrant.* Published monthly, it is free, comprehensive and widely available. The Tourist Board publishes *Day by Day*, a useful monthly information and listings magazine in English – on sale in newsagents, but you can pick it up free in hotels and restaurants.

8 AUB Ticketshop

For information on plays and concerts, or to make reservations (for a small fee), phone or visit the Amsterdam Uitburo ticketshop. 🖝 *Leidseplein 26 • Map C5 • 0900 0191*

9 Newspapers

You will find the best selection of foreign daily and Sunday newspapers at Athenaeum Nieuwscentrum, Waterstone's and the American Book Center. 🖝 *Athenaeum Nieuwscentrum: Spui 14–16. Map M5 • Waterstone's: Kalverstraat 152. Map M5 • American Book Center: Kalverstraat 185. Map M5*

10 Libraries

Only residents can borrow, but anyone can visit a public library for reference purposes. The Centrale Bibliotheek is handy, with a good range of foreign-language books and newspapers – as well as a café. 🖝 *Prinsengracht 587 • Map K5 • 020 523 0900 • Open 1–9pm Mon, 10am–9pm Tue–Thu, 10am–5pm Fri–Sat; Apr–Oct: 1–5pm Sun*

For alternative listings, pick up Shark *free from the AUB Ticketshop; also online at www.underwateramsterdam.com*

Left **Bicycles secured in a bike rack** Right **Trams**

10 Getting Around

1 Trams

The tram is Amsterdam's most popular mode of transport. Trams run from 6am (6:30am on Saturday and Sunday) till midnight. Most start at Centraal Station. For routes, see the map on the back cover of this book. You can buy tickets in advance from the GVB (see below), or on board the tram itself – from the driver, the conductor or a ticket machine.

2 Buses

Like trams, most buses start at Centraal Station. A few follow similar routes, but buses also go to areas not covered by the tram network; again, see the map on the back cover. Buses have the same ticketing system as trams. A limited night bus service runs from midnight to 4am.

3 Metro

Serving more remote parts of the city, the metro has only three lines, all terminating at Centraal Station. There are four other stations in the central area: Amsterdam CS, Nieuwmarkt, Waterlooplein and Weesperplein. It is best to avoid taking the metro at night, when the stations are haunts of unsavoury characters.

4 Tickets

The cheapest way to travel by tram, bus or metro is to buy a *strippenkaart* (ticket strip available in multiples of 15), a *dagkaart* (day ticket), or a *sterabonnement* (season ticket) – all sold by the public transport authority, the GVB *(Gemeente Vervoer Bedrijf)*, tourist offices and some newsagents. ◎ *GVB: Stationsplein 14 • Map P1 • 0900 9292*

5 Taxis

You cannot hail taxis in the street, but finding one in the centre is usually easy, as there are plenty of taxi ranks: at Centraal Station, Dam Square, Elandsgracht, Leidseplein, Muziektheater, Nieuwmarkt and Rembrantsplein. There is also a 24-hour phone service, Taxicentrale. ◎ *Taxicentrale: 020 677 7777*

6 Driving

The city centre has a complex one-way system, its roads are dominated by trams and cyclists, and parking is limited – and expensive. All of these are good reasons to avoid driving. If you have to, park in a car park *(see p133)* or on a meter (most allow you up to two hours). If you overstay your time, your car might be clamped or towed away. Don't leave valuables in your car.

7 Bicycle Hire

You will never be very far from a bicycle hire shop in this city of cyclists: Bike City, Holland Rent-a-Bike and Take-a-Bike are all conveniently central. Bike theft is rife, so secure your bike carefully when you park it. ◎ *Bike City: Bloemgracht 68. Map K2. 020 626 3721 • Holland Rent-a-Bike · Damrak 247 · Map N2 · 020 622 3207 • Macbike: Stationsplein 12. Map P1. 020 624 8391*

8 Canal Bikes

If you are fit, these two- or four-person pedaloes provide a fun – if laborious – way of getting around. There are four moorings in central Amsterdam, where you can collect or leave the bikes all year round. ◎ *Canal Bike: Weteringschans 24 • Map D5 • 020 626 5574*

9 Trains

Nederlandse Spoorwegen, the Dutch national rail company, is renowned for its clean, punctual trains and reasonable fares. Contact the OVR (Openbaar Vervoer Reisinformatie) for information. ◎ *OVR: 0900 9292 • www.ns.nl*

10 Walking

Amsterdam is a great city for walking *(see pp64–5)*. The main pedestrian hazards are bicycles, trams and cobbled streets, so keep clear of cycle lanes, take care crossing tram tracks, and wear comfortable, flat shoes.

For a tram or bus journey within one zone, you must use two strips of a strippenkaart per person. Two zones require three strips.

135

Left **Canal tour** Right **Tram on the Circle route**

TOP 10 Sightseeing

1 Amsterdam Pass
Available from hotels and Amsterdam Tourist Board offices *(see p134)*, the Amsterdam pass represents good value for money, at €26, €36 and €46 for one, two and three days respectively. It entitles the holder to free public transport, free admission to many museums, a free canal tour, and discounts at a variety of restaurants and other attractions.

2 Museumjaarkaart
Most of the top museums are covered by the Amsterdam Pass *(see above)*. If you want to visit more, you need the *Museumjaarkaart* (Museum Card), which buys a year's admission to over 400 museums throughout the Netherlands. You will recoup the cost after about ten visits. Available from Amsterdam Tourist Board offices and all participating museums.

3 Cultureel Jongeren Passport (CJP)
The CJP gives under-26-year-olds discounted admission to theatres, museums and other attractions. It is available from offices of the Amsterdam Tourist Board and the AUB Uitburo ticketshop *(see p134)*.

4 Canal Tours
Cruises around Amsterdam's canals can either be booked direct

with the operator or through the Amsterdam Tourist Board. Many operators – including the well-reputed Lovers – start from Centraal Station. Amsterdam Canal Cruises start on Singelgracht, and Kooij from Rokin, near the Munttoren. ◊ *Lovers: Prins Hendrikkade 26. Map P1. 020 530 1090 • Amsterdam Canal Cruises: Nicolaas Witsenkade 1a. Map D6. 020 626 5636 • Kooij: Rokin 125. Map N5. 020 623 3810*

5 Museum Boat
The Museum Boat allows you to get on and off at any of six different points to visit the major museums. The day ticket also entitles you to discounted admission. A boat comes by each stop once every 30 minutes between 10am and 5pm Tue to Sun. ◊ *Stationsplein 8 • Map P1 • 020 530 1090*

6 Canalbus
Another frequent hop-on, hop-off canal boat, with discounts included in the ticket price. Choose one of three routes, with a total of eleven stops. An inexpensive one-day All Amsterdam Transport Pass entitles you to unlimited use of metro, bus, tram and Canalbus. ◊ *Weteringschans 24 • Map D5 • 020 623 9886*

7 Water Taxi
More private cruisers than taxis, these make a

fun way of seeing the canals if you are in a group and can share the cost, which is around €120 an hour for an 8-seater. ◊ *Stationsplein 8 • Map P1 • 020 530 1090*

8 Circle Tram
The Circle Tram No. 20 starts from Centraal Station. You can stay on board all the way or – if you have a day pass – jump on and off.

9 Bicycle Tours
Yellow Bike offers two guided bicycle tours for up to 12 people: a three-hour city tour and a six-hour countryside tour. You can book direct through Yellow Bike, or through the Amsterdam Tourist Board. ◊ *Yellow Bike: 020 620 6940*

10 Walking Tours
The Amsterdam Tourist Board offers a range of walking tours; they also have leaflets on self-guided walks. Urban Home & Garden Tours visit private and public canal houses with lunch or tea. Mee in Mokum give fresh insights into historic Amsterdam, while Archivisie concentrate on architectural heritage. Audiotourist offer three walks with commentary on personal stereo. ◊ *Urban Home & Garden Tours: 020 688 1243 • Mee in Mokum: 020 625 1390 • Archivisie: 020 625 8908 • Audiotourist: 020 421 5580*

ft Street stall selling herring Right **Street performer**

10 Amsterdam on a Budget

1 Hostels and Camping

here are several popular uth hostels (see box). ondelpark is especially commended, with ivate rooms as well as ormitories. Vliegenbos a designated youth mpsite. The Amster- ımse Bos campsite also ıs wooden cabins for re, and, like Gaasper, is ited to families. (See so Budget Hotels, p149.)

2 Discount Cards

Under-26-year-olds n apply for a CJP for rgains on some per- rming arts tickets (see 136). The Amsterdam ıss represents good lue for money. The useumjaarkaart allows ee admission to more an 400 museums in the etherlands (see p136).

3 Public Transport

A strippenkaart (see 135) is better value than ıgle tram tickets. The msterdam Pass (see 136) includes free public ınsport. The All Amster- ım Transport Pass buys ɔu a day's unlimited use the transport system.

4 Markets

The outdoor markets Albert Cuypmarkt, 'aterlooplein and ɔordermarkt, and the door bargain basement ɔmmelmarkt, are all aces where you can find food, clothing and ic-a-brac for next to ɔthing (see p62).

5 Free Sights

Special places that can be visited free of charge include: the Civic Guards Gallery of the Amsterdams Historisch Museum (see p26); hofjes (see p92); the Begijnhof (see p22); Hollandse Manege (see p117); the Rijksmuseum Garden (see p14); and Bloemenmarkt (see p109).

6 Free Music

There is plenty of music in the air, from the carillons of the Wester- toren, Zuidertoren and Munttoren, to barrel organs, street performers and live bands in late- night bars. Free lunch- time concerts are held at the Concertgebouw (Wed), Stopera (Tue in winter), English Reformed Church (summer) and Thomas- kerk (alternate Tuesdays).

7 Free Film and Theatre

There are free perform- ances at the Vondelpark's open-air theatre, and free screenings in summer at the Nederlands Film- museum (see p116).

8 Tickets

To see what's on, consult Uitkrant and Day by Day. The best place to book tickets is AUB in Leidseplein (see p134).

9 Parks

Amsterdam's parks offer endless free enter- tainment, from theatre and concerts in the Vondelpark to the miniature train in Amstelpark, or just feeding the goats in Amsterdamse Bos.

10 Cheap Eats

You can keep hunger at bay without entering a restaurant in Amsterdam, with its many food stalls selling raw herring, smoked fish, chips with mayonnaise, belegde broodjes (filled bread rolls), waffles, pancakes and delicious, sugary poffertjes – and there are plenty of cheap cafés.

Hostels and Campsites

Hans Brinker
Kerkstraat 136 • 020 622 0687

The Bulldog
Oude Zijds Voorburgwal 220 • 020 620 3822

Flying Pig Palace
Vossiusstraat 4 • 020 400 4187

NJHC Vondelpark
Zandpad 5 • 020 589 8996

Amsterdamse Bos Camping
Kleine Noorddijk 1, Amstelveen • 020 641 6868

Gaasper Camping
Loosdrechtdreef 7 • 020 696 7326

Vliegenbos Camping
Meeuwenlaan 138 • 020 636 8855

Left **Cheese on a stall in the Albert Cuypmarkt** Right **Tulips at Amsterdam's Bloemenmarkt**

🔟 Shopping Tips

1 Areas
Each of Amsterdam's shopping areas has its own special character. De Negen Straatjes, the Jordaan and Haarlemmerbuurt have clusters of charming bric-a-brac and speciality shops. The Spiegelkwartier and Rokin are the places to hunt for art and antiques. Most of the chain stores are located in Kalverstraat and Nieuwendijk. Leidsestraat and Utrechtsestraat have more upmarket boutiques and PC Hooftstraat is the home of designer fashion.

2 Hours
Shops are generally open from 9am–6pm Tue, Wed and Fri, from 9am–9pm on Thu, from 9am–5pm on Sat, and from 1–6pm on Mon (although most department stores open at 11am). Many shops also open from noon to 6pm on Sun. By city law, shopkeepers can trade between 7am and 10pm daily.

3 Tax-free Shopping
Most marked prices include 19 per cent VAT. Non-EU residents are entitled to a refund of 13.5 per cent on goods costing more than €135, bought at one shop on the same day and exported within 30 days. If the shop has 'Tax-free' status, collect a Global Refund Cheque, have it stamped by Customs on your departure, and claim your refund when you leave the EU.

4 Sales
January and July are the traditional months for end-of-season sales, when you are likely to find some great bargains. Some shops have an almost permanent sale rail. *Korting* means reductions are being offered. The Dutch for sale is *uitverkoop*.

5 What to Buy
Amsterdam shopping is very cosmopolitan. It spans designer fashion and off-beat second-hand clothes, valuable antiques and colourful Indonesian beads. For a flavour of the city, you might be tempted by Dutch chocolate, cheese, *paling* (raw herring), beer or *jenever* or, for something less ephemeral, Delftware or diamonds.

6 Department Stores and Malls
Compared to its speciality shops, Amsterdam's department stores seem run-of-the-mill. On the corner of Dam Square and Damrak, De Bijenkorf is the most famous. More exclusive, however, are Maison de Bonneterie and Metz & Co. The city's first mall, Magna Plaza, has several floors of boutiques and cafés in a converted post office.

7 Speciality Shops
It is these quirky little shops devoted to specific items – from candles to toothbrushes – that make shopping in Amsterdam such a joy. Although the crop up throughout the city, they are thickest on the ground in De Negen Straatjes *(see p104)*.

8 Art and Antiques
The Spiegelkwartier is the heart of the art an antiques trade. Here, a host of dealers specializ in a variety of objects from Delftware and glas to icons and tribal art *(see p112)*.

9 Diamonds
The five members o the Amsterdam Diamon Foundation guarantee quality. ⓢ *Amsterdam Diamond Center: Rokin 1. Map N3. 020 624 5787 • Coster Diamonds: Paulus Potterstraat 2–6. Map C5. 020 305 5555 • Gassan Diamonds: Nieuwe Uilenburgerstraat 173–5. Map Q4. 020 622 5333 • Stoelt Diamonds: Wagenstraat 13–17. Map P6. 020 623 7601 • Van Moppes Diamonds: Albert Cuypstraat 2–6. Map D6. 020 676 1242*

🔟 Bulbs and Flower
The Dutch love flowers. For the best selection of cut flowers and bulbs, go to the Bloemenmarkt *(see p113)*. Depending on the harshness of the winter bulbs are usually available between June and late December, but chee your own country's import regulations befor exporting *(see p132)*.

Left **Boonstra taxi service** Right **Disabled access sign**

10 Amsterdam for the Disabled

1 Organizations
Amsterdam's narrow, cobbled streets, uneven pavements, and old buildings with small entrances and steep stairs, make it a difficult city for disabled people to get around. For general information and advice, contact Mobility International, Chronisch Zieken & Gehandicapten-raad Nederland or SIG (Stichting Informatie Gehandicapten). ✆ *Mobility International: Postbus 532, 6800 AM Arnhem. 026 370 6161 • Chronisch Zieken & Gehandicaptenraad Nederland: Postbus 196, 3500 AD Utrecht. 030 297 9404 • SIG: Postbus 19152, 3501 DD Utrecht. 030 230 6603*

2 Leaflets
Useful leaflets on hotels, restaurants, museums and attractions, guided tours and excursions for people with disabilities are available from the Amsterdam Tourist Office and the AUB (Amsterdam Uitburo) *(see p134)*. You can also pick up an excellent booklet called Rail Travel for the Disabled from Centraal Station.

3 Accommodation
For such a progressive city, Amsterdam's hotels are remarkably cavalier about the needs of disabled people; very few have special facilities. Some modern hotels have adapted rooms, but old buildings and converted canal houses often have steep staircases and no lift. The accommodation booklet of the Amsterdam Tourist Office indicates hotels with disabled facilities, but be sure that they meet your needs before you make a reservation.

4 Public Transport
Old-style trams with high steps are inaccessible to wheelchair users. New trams are more accessible, with central doors at pavement level. The metro is wheelchair-friendly, with lifts at every station. For the visually impaired, there is a conductor who announces every stop. Avoid public transport at rush hour.

5 Taxis
A folded wheelchair will fit into most taxis, but Amsterdam has a private service, Boonstra, specially designed for wheelchair users. It costs the same as a regular cab, but you need to book at least 24 hours in advance. ✆ *Prins Bernhardkade 1, Halfweg • 020 613 4134 • 9am–6pm Mon to Sat*

6 Museums
Most of the city's principal museums have adequate facilities for disabled people, including wide entrances, ramps, lifts and adapted toilets, although canal-house museums like the Amstelkring, Van Loon and Willet-Holthuysen have no upper-floor wheelchair access. Staff are usually very helpful, but it's always a good idea to telephone before you visit.

7 Restaurants
It's possible to get a wheelchair into most ground-floor restaurants, but only a handful have disabled toilet facilities. Once again, the best advice is to phone ahead.

8 Wheelchair Hire
You can rent a wheelchair from Beumer de Jong for €20 per week, but you have to arrange for your hotel to collect it. Book well in advance, particularly in the holiday season. ✆ *Haarlemmermeerstraat 49–51 • 020 615 7188*

9 Guided Tours
Stichting Recreatie Gehandicapten organizes trips to and around Amsterdam, and elsewhere in Holland. ✆ *Postbus 4140, 2003 EC Haarlem • 023 536 8409*

10 Impaired Sight
Improvements have been made for blind and partially sighted travellers, including audio tours of museums and other tourist attractions, and the publication of a railway timetable in Braille, available from the Library for the Blind. ✆ *0486 486 486*

Left **Pedestrian-free cycle lane** Right **Queue at Rijksmuseum**

Things to Avoid

1 Street Crime
Beware pickpockets in crowded places like Centraal Station, the Red Light District, Damrak and Leidseplein. Never keep money in your back pocket, or leave your handbag exposed. At night, avoid the junkie-riddled fringes of the Red Light District, especially around sleazy Zeedijk, as well as the area around Nieuwendijk between Damrak and Spuistraat.

2 Bicycle Theft
Bicycle theft is rife in Amsterdam. Some are stolen for profit, others on the principle that "someone stole mine, so I'll steal someone else's". Always secure both front wheel and frame to an immovable object with a U-shaped lock.

3 Medical Problems
EU nationals are entitled to receive dental and medical treatment in the Netherlands at a reduced charge. To cover this, British visitors should bring a form E111, available from post offices. It is also sensible to take out private travel insurance before you leave, to cover medical emergencies and repatriation (see p142).

4 Dog Mess
It's a strange paradox that the famously house-proud Dutch should put up with fouled streets in their capital city (other towns and cities are much cleaner). A few years ago the problem was dire; it's much better now, but you still need to look where you walk.

5 Losing Possessions
If you lose property at Schiphol Airport, call 020 601 2349. For items left on a train, call 030 235 3923, 8am–8pm Mon–Fri, 9am–5pm Sat. For trams, buses or the metro, call 020 460 5858, 9am–4:30pm Mon–Fri.

6 Infringing Drug Laws
Amsterdam's enlightened attitude to soft drugs should not be misconstrued. "Coffee shops" are the only places where buying and using small quantities of soft drugs is tolerated. Elsewhere – in the street, or in other bars and cafés – smoking is frowned on.

7 Causing Offence
As the expression "going Dutch" indicates, Amsterdammers will usually share the bill in a restaurant. If you dine at someone's home, bring a small gift such as flowers or chocolates for the host. Try not to annoy cyclists by walking in cycle lanes. Though most Amsterdammers speak excellent English, a few words in Dutch will go down well (see pp158–9). In the Red Light District, don't cause offence by taking photographs of the prostitutes in their windows.

8 Mosquitoes
Summertime heralds the arrival of these irritating insects, attracted to the canal waters. Arm yourself with the repellent and bite creams of your choice.

9 Getting Caught Short
Though there are (albeit very public) men's conveniences on some streets, women are very poorly provided for. Instead, it is acceptable practice to head for the nearest bar or café. You might buy a drink in return, but usually you are not obliged to. Public toilets in stations and museums are staffed by attendants who insist on a tip in a saucer.

10 Tourist Hordes
Amsterdam is busy all year round, but especially from April to September, when you should book up your accommodation well before you plan to visit. Canal cruises and other tours should be booked on arrival. Places like the Rijksmuseum and Anne Frankhuis attract long queues. Arrive early, and in the case of the Rijksmuseum, use the back (Hobbemastraat) entrance if necessary. Crowded trams just have to be endured.

ft **EasyEverything internet café** Right **Post Office**

10 Banking and Communications

1 Currency

In January 2002, the Dutch guilder became obsolete and the euro became the official currency of the Netherlands. Euro banknotes have seven denominations: 5, 10, 20, 50, 100, 200 and 500. There are also eight coin denominations: 1 and 2 euros, and 1, 2, 5, 10, 20 and 50 cents. Check exchange rates before you travel.

2 Credit Cards

Major cards including Amex are widely accepted throughout Amsterdam, and you should have no difficulty paying for most things with plastic – but is always wise to check. Some restaurants do not accept credit cards, and is common practice to pay small amounts in cash, so you should keep some on you.

3 Cash Dispensers

Amsterdam has no shortage of cash dispensers, many of which will function in several languages.

4 Travellers' Cheques

Travellers' cheques are a safe way of carrying money abroad, and can be exchanged for cash in banks and used to pay hotel bills, as well as being widely accepted in retail outlets. Choose a well-known company such as American Express or Thomas Cook.

5 Changing Money

You can change money in banks, bureaux de change, post offices and American Express offices. To avoid high commission charges, stay clear of independent bureaux de change (like those on Leidsestraat) and choose the official GWK bureaux de change or the post office Postbank. Avoid changing money in hotels.

6 Post Offices

Amsterdam's post offices are recognizable by their TPG logo. Apart from the usual services, they also change currency and travellers' cheques. The main post office on Singel has a poste restante service, parcel service, photocopiers and a philately counter. ✆ Singel 250 • Map M3 • 020 330 0555 • open 9am–6pm Mon–Wed & Fri, 9am–8pm Thu, 10am–1.30pm Sat

7 Internet Cafés

You can pick up and send emails, or just surf the web, at any time of the day or night at EasyEverything – the Reguliersbreestraat branch has an astonishing 300 terminals. There are several other internet cafés in town, and some hotels and bars also have terminals. ✆ EasyEverything: Reguliersbreestraat 22/Damrak 33. Map N6/Map P2. Open 24 hours daily • Cyber Café: Nieuwendijk 19. Map N1. Open 10am–1am Sun–Thu, 10am–3am Fri–Sat • De Waag: Nieuwmarkt 4. Map P3. Open 10am–1am daily

8 Telephones

Most public telephones (which are green, with the KPN Telecom logo) require a phonecard – which you can buy at post offices, supermarkets, newsagents and stations – or credit card. The international dialling code for The Netherlands is 00 31. The code for Amsterdam is 020 – you can drop this if you are dialling a local number.

9 Television

Ask a Dutch child where he or she learned to speak such good, idiomatic English, and the answer is likely to be "from the television". British and American imports on Dutch channels are subtitled rather than dubbed, and cable TV brings about 20 stations from around Europe, plus America's CNN. Most hotels are equipped with cable TV.

10 Radio

For classical music, tune in to Dutch Radio 4 (98.9 MHz); for pop music to Radio 3 (96.8 MHz). There are also several independent music stations, mostly aimed at the young. News is broadcast on Radio 1 (747 kHz).

Left **Prescriptions at an *apotheek*** Right **A&E dept, Onze Lieve Vrouwe Gasthuis**

🔟 Security and Health

1 Emergency
Dial 112 if you need police, ambulance or fire brigade. English-speaking operators man the 24-hour switchboard, and you can phone free from a call box.

2 Personal Safety
Crime affecting visitors tends to be petty theft by pickpockets and bag-snatchers, so don't carry your passport, ticket and other valuables around with you. At night, stick to well-lit streets, avoiding dodgy areas like De Pijp, Nieuwendijk and the seediest part of the Red Light District around Zeedijk.

3 Theft
Make sure that your possessions are insured before you travel. Should you have anything stolen, report it immediately to the nearest police station and ask for a copy of the police report for your insurers. If your passport is stolen, you must also contact your consulate *(see below)*.

4 Police
The Amsterdam police have a reputation for being friendly and helpful. Their headquarters, the Hoofdbureau van Politie, is in Elandsgracht. There are main police stations in Prinsengracht, Beursstraat and Lijnbaansgracht. ✆ *Elandsgracht 117. Map J5 • Prinsengracht 1109. Map E5 • Beursstraat 33. Map*

P2 • Lijnbaansgracht 219. Map C5 • 0900 8844 (central no.)

5 Victim Support
If you are a victim of crime, you can get help from the Amsterdam Tourist Assistance Service (ATAS), which offers support and practical advice. De Eerste Lijn helps victims of rape and sexual assault. ✆ *Amsterdam Tourist Assistance Service: Nieuwezijds Voorburgwal 104–8. 020 625 3246 • De Eerste Lijn. 020 613 0245*

6 Hospitals
Of the central hospitals, only one, Onze Lieve Vrouwe Gasthuis, has an accident and emergency department. ✆ *Onze Lieve Vrouwe Gasthuis • 1e Oosterparkstraat 279 • 020 599 9111*

7 Pharmacies
For non-prescription drugs or toiletries, go to a chemist *(drogist)*. To have a prescription made up, go to a pharmacy *(apotheek)*. Normal opening times are 8:30am–5:30pm Mon–Fri. A notice in the window will direct you to the nearest pharmacy open outside of these hours.

8 Doctors and Dentists
If you have raging earache or toothache, your hotel, local pharmacy or tourist office will give you the name and address of an

English-speaking doctor or dentist, as will the Central Medical Service *(Centrale Doktersdienst)*. EU citizens are entitled to reductions on medical and dental treatment *(see p140)*. ✆ *Central Medical Service: 020 592 3434*

9 Embassies and Consulates
If you lose your passport or get into trouble with the authorities, you will need to contact your embassy or consulate. Most embassies are in The Hague, but some countries, including the UK and the USA, have consular facilities in Amsterdam. ✆ *UK Consulate: Koningslaan 44. 020 676 4343 • US Consulate: Museumplein 19. 020 575 5309*

10 Sexual Health
The Dutch take sexual health seriously: prostitutes are subjected to rigorous checks to ensure that they remain healthy. Should you contract a sexually transmitted disease, the GG&GD provides a Mon–Fri walk-in clinic; phone for details or an appointment. An HIV clinic run by SAD Schorerstichting is held here on Friday evenings. An AIDS Helpline operates 2–10pm Mon–Fri. ✆ *GG&GD: Groenburgwal 4. Map P5. 020 555 5822 • SAD Schorerstichting: 020 662 4206 • AIDS-STD Helpline: 0900 204 2040*

Left **Inside the UvA Main Library** Right **VU Boekhandel**

10 Amsterdam for Students

1 UvA Courses

The largest university with buildings in the centre, UvA (Universiteit van Amsterdam) offers English-language international Study Programs in a range of subjects from under-graduate level upwards. For information, contact the Office of Foreign Relations. ✆ *Office of Foreign Relations: Binnengasthuisstraat 9 • Map N5 • 020 525 8080*

2 VU Courses

In a suburb of Amsterdam, VU (Vrije Universiteit) runs English-language courses in economics, law, arts and social sciences for exchange or contract students (whose home university has no official exchange relationship with the VU). ✆ *VU Student Information: 020 444 5000*

3 Accommodation

UvA's Housing Department helps students find lodgings. If you are studying at VU, the university has a guesthouse in Uilenstede. Alternatively, SRVU, the VU students' union, will help you. ✆ *UvA Housing Department: Binnengasthuisstraat 9. Map N5. 020 525 2744 • SRVU: De Boelelaan 1183A. 020 444 9424*

4 Student Cards

Producing your student union or ISIC rail-card in Amsterdam is no guarantee of discounted prices, and only Dutch students are entitled to the *OV Jaarkaart*, which gives them free use of public transport. Anyone under the age of 26 is eligible for a *Cultureel Jongeren Passport (see p136)*, which costs €11 from Tourist Offices or the AUB *(see p134)*.

5 Unions

Foreign students will find ASVA-OBAS the most useful of the various Dutch student unions. It offers all kinds of assistance, including an accommodation service. SRVU will also give VU students help and advice *(see above)*. ✆ *ASVA-OBAS: Binnengasthuisstraat 9 • Map N5 • 020 623 8052*

6 Services for Foreign Students

An independent organization, the FSS (Foreign Student Service) provides advice, support and help for foreign students, as well as arranging social events. Under the auspices of the UvA, the International Student Network (ISN) is a group of students that provides mentors to introduce foreigners and freshmen to university life. ✆ *FSS: UK Consulate, Koningslaan 44. 020 676 4343. US Consulate, Museumplein 19. 020 575 5309 • ISN: 020 525 3721. isn@stuc.uva.nl. www.stuc.uva.nl/isn*

7 Summer University

Every year, from the middle of July to the beginning of September, the Amsterdam Summer University offers arts and sciences courses in the Felix Meritis Building. ✆ *Keizersgracht 324 • Map L4 • 020 620 0225 • www. amsu.edu*

8 Bookshops

Most major book-shops stock English textbooks, but the best academic bookshop is VU Boekhandel. ✆ *VU Boek-handel: De Boelelaan 1105 • 020 644 4355*

9 Libraries

To borrow from the UvA Main Library, you need a *Universiteit Bibliotheek* card. Foreign students are eligible if they are studying in the city for at least three months. To borrow from the VU Main Library, you must become a member. ✆ *UvA Main Library: Singel 425. Map M5. 020 525 2266 • VU Main Library: De Boelelaan 1105. 020 444 5200*

10 Visas

All foreign students who plan to stay in the country for longer than three months must register with the *Vreemdelingen Politie* (Aliens Police) within three days of arrival. They must then apply for a VTV (residence permit) and register with the civil registry.

Left **Crown Plaza Amsterdam American** Right **Grand Hotel Krasnapolsky**

🔟 Luxury Hotels

1 Amstel Inter-Continental

Rub shoulders with monarchs and movie stars in Amsterdam's grandest hotel, which just oozes opulence, from the spectacular hall to the pampering bedrooms. Enjoy the state-of-the-art gym, private motor launch and Michelin-starred restaurant – but don't even think about the bill. ✎ *Professor Tulpplein 1, 1018 GX · Map F5 · 020 622 6060 · www. interconti.com · Dis. access · €€€€€*

2 Blakes

British designer Anouska Hempel has taken a Catholic almshouse and turned it into a glamorous hotel with an excellent restaurant *(see p103)*. Influenced by Asia, the theme is monochrome, with gorgeous fabrics and furnishings. ✎ *Keizersgracht 384, 1016 GB · Map L4 · 020 530 2010 · www.blakes-amsterdam. com · €€€€€*

3 Grand Amsterdam (Sofitel Demeure)

A sense of history pervades this hotel on the fringes of the Red Light District: the 17th-century building was designed for the Admiralty. It offers five-star comfort and is home to Café Roux *(see p60)*. ✎ *Oudezijds Voorburgwal 197, 1012 EX · Map N4 · 020 555 3111 · www.thegrand.nl · Dis. access · €€€€€*

4 Pulitzer

Combining 21st-century chic with beams and bare bricks, the Pulitzer is an innovative conversion of 24 canal houses, celebrated for its art exhibitions, courtyard garden and outstanding cellar. ✎ *Prinsengracht 315–31, 1016 GZ · Map K3 · 020 523 5235 · www. starwoodhotels.com · €€€€€*

5 NH Grand Hotel Krasnapolsky

This monumental hotel, with 469 rooms and 36 apartments, has come a long way from its beginnings as a humble coffee shop *(see p35)*. The facilities are phenomenal. Of the four restaurants, the original cast-iron and glass Winter Garden is the most stunning. ✎ *Dam 9, 1012 JS · Map N3 · 020 554 9111 · www. nh-hotels.com · Dis.access · €€€*

6 De l'Europe

Once through the door, you leave the hurly-burly of the Nieuwe Zijde behind and enter a calm oasis redolent of the 19th century. Spacious rooms with empire furnishings are the epitome of plush. ✎ *Nieuwe Doelenstraat 2–8, 1012 CP · Map N5 · 020 531 1777 · www.leurope.nl · Dis.access · €€€€€*

7 NH Barbizon Palace

Behind a dull façade, a row of 17th-century houses – 19 in all – have been knocked together t create a luxurious hotel. ✎ *Prins Hendrikkade 59–72 1012 AD · Map P1 · 020 556 4564 · www.nh-hotels com · Dis.access · €€€€€*

8 Crowne Plaza Amsterdam American

This landmark hotel in a splendid Art Nouveau building is for those who want to be close to the action *(see p101)*. ✎ *Leidsekade 97, 1017 PN · Map C5 · 020 556 3000 · www.amsterdam-american crowneplaza.com · Dis.access · €€€€€*

9 Bilderberg Jan Luyken

A step from the main museums and elegant shopping, this four-star boutique hotel comprises three stylish 19th-century townhouses. Treats include free afternoon te and a charming terrace. ✎ *Jan Luykenstraat 58, 1071 CS · Map C5 · 020 573 0730 · www.janluyken.nl Dis.access · €€€€*

10 Bilderberg Garden

For luxury away from the crowds, this modern hotel in a leafy street might fit the bill. With 124 rooms and suites, all with relaxing Jacuzzi baths, it's smaller than many of the city's five-stars, with a friendly atmosphere. ✎ *Dijsselhof plantsoen 7, 1077 BJ · 020 570 5600 · www.garden hotel.nl · €€€€€*

Note: *Unless otherwise stated, all hotels accept credit cards and have en-suite bathrooms.*

Price Categories

For a standard,
double room per
night (with breakfast
if included), taxes
and extra charges.

€ under €90
€€ €90–140
€€€ €140–200
€€€€ €200–250
€€€€€ over €250

Canal House salon

🔟 Hotels with Character

1 Canal House
The Golden Age lives
in this tranquil pair of
17th-century canal
houses, filled from top to
bottom with antiques.
Breakfast beneath a
chandelier in the ornate
salon with a view of the
garden. The bedrooms
are individually decorated
and priced). ✆ Keizers-
gracht 148, 1015 CX • Map
2 • 020 622 5182 •
www.canalhouse.nl • €€€

2 Ambassade
Overlooking the
Herengracht, the
Ambassade is truly
comfortable and, not
surprisingly, often full.
Rambling through ten
handsome merchant's
houses, it blends good
antiques with excellent
modern service. Popular
with writers, the new
library showcases signed
copies of their work. ✆
Herengracht 341, 1016 AZ •
Map L4 · 020 555 0222 •
www.ambassade-hotel.nl •
€€

3 Seven Bridges
A tired bridge-spotter
can count seven from
this charming hotel
without moving. Immac-
ately decorated, it has
wooden floors, Persian
carpets and furniture that
would grace any auction-
house catalogue. There
are no public rooms, so
you can have breakfast in
bed without a twinge of
guilt. ✆ Reguliersgracht 31,
1017 LK • Map E5 • 020
623 1329 • €€

4 De Filosoof
This unique hotel's
love affair with philosophy
goes beyond its name:
philosophers stay and
meet here regularly. ✆
Anna van den Vondelstraat
6, 1054 GZ • Map B5 •
020 683 3013 • www.
hotelfilosoof.nl • Dis.
access • €€

5 Amsterdam Wiechmann
Made from three well-
kept canal houses, the
Wiechmann has been
polishing its welcome
for more than 50 years.
Wooden floors, beams
and panelling set off
antique furniture and
Oriental rugs, and the
bedrooms, most with
canal views, are
attractively simple.
✆ Prinsengracht 328–32,
1016 HX • Map K4 • 020
626 3321 • www.
hotelwiechmann.nl • €€

6 Prinsenhof
This small, quiet B&B
in an attractive canal
house is squeaky clean,
friendly and modestly
priced. Small wonder,
then that its 10 pretty
bedrooms (some with
shared facilities) are hard
to come by. ✆ Prinsen-
gracht 810, 1017 JL • Map
E5 • 020 623 1772 • www.
hotelprinsenhof.com • €

7 Seven One Seven
This is a luxuriously
laid-back hotel in a five-
star neighbourhood,
where beautiful antiques
complement the even
more beautiful guests. To
simplify your bill, breakfast, tea and evening
drinks are included in the
cost of the accom-
modation. ✆ Prinsengracht
717, 1017 JW • Map E5 •
020 427 0717 • www.
717hotel.nl • €€€€€

8 Toro
There is a decidedly
English air about this
elegant, plant-filled villa
south of the Vondelpark.
The public rooms are
furnished with antiques
and oil paintings, and you
can take tea in the
delightful garden. ✆
Koningslaan 64, 1075 AG •
Map A6 • 020 673 7223 •
info@ams.nl • www.ams.nl
• Dis.access • €€€

9 Toren
Recently renovated,
this graceful but comfortable 17th-century canal
house has all the modern
technology you could
wish for, and at modest
prices. ✆ Keizersgracht
164, 1015 CZ • Map L2 •
020 622 6352 • www.
toren.nl • €€

🔟 Agora
Overlooking the
Singel and conveniently
close to the huge floating
flower market, this small,
intimate hotel also has a
peaceful garden. Wooden
beams, good furniture,
new bathrooms and
reasonable rates are hard
to resist. ✆ Singel 462,
1017 AW • Map M5 • 020
627 2200 • www.hotel
agora.nl • €€

Left **Rembrandt** Right **Schiller**

Family Hotels

1 Owl
Although there are no particular facilities for children (beyond triple rooms and cots for babies), this family-run hotel in the Museum Quarter is noted for its friendliness. A stuffed owl in an alcove provides the name. The hotel has a neat little garden, and fresh flowers in the fairly plain rooms. ✪ *Roemer Visscherstraat 1, 1054 EV • Map C5 • 020 618 9484 • manager@owl-hotel.demon. nl • €€*

2 Adolesce
Cheerful, friendly and simple, this canal house in Plantage has a welcoming attitude to children, with family rooms. Breakfast is no longer served (there are places nearby) but hot and cold drinks, fruit and cookies are on offer during the day. ✪ *Nieuwe Kiezersgracht 26, 1018 DS • Map R6 • 020 626 3959 • adolesce@xs4all.nl • €€*

3 Singel
Animal-loving children will enjoy staying opposite the Poezenboot *(see p10)*. The family-run hotel has an excellent location on a pretty stretch of the Singel, and small but characterful bedrooms. Under-seven-year olds stay for free, and babysitting can be arranged. ✪ *Singel 13, 1012 VC • Map N1 • 020 626 3108 • www.lempereur-hotels.nl • Dis. access • €€€*

4 Amsterdam House
Treat the children to life aboard a houseboat. Amsterdam House has eight of them available for short or long rentals, as well as apartments and hotel rooms. ✪ *'s-Gravelandse Veer 3–4, 1011 KM• Map N5 • 020 626 2577 • www.amster damhouse.com • €€*

5 Estheréa
In the same family for three generations, this elegant hotel mixes modern facilities with traditional surroundings and a warm atmosphere. Bedrooms, including family rooms, are fresh and well-equipped. Baby baths and high chairs are available, and babysitting. ✪ *Singel 303, 1012 WJ • Map M4 • 020 624 5146 • www.estherea.nl • €€€€*

6 't Jagershuis
This small waterfront inn is a good option for families who prefer to stay outside the city centre. Just 10 km (6 miles) from the city by bus or bicycle, it's in a charming village *(see p128)* and there are family rooms. ✪ *Amstelzijde 2-4, 1184 VA Ouderkerk aan de Amstel • 020 496 2020 • www.jagershuis.com • Dis. access • €€€*

7 Wihelmina
Recently renovated, this is an excellent two-star hotel in the Museum Quarter, with three- and

four-bedded rooms. The yellow breakfast room is particularly jolly. ✪ *Koninginneweg 167, 1075 CN • 020 662 5467 • www hotelwilhelmina.com • €€*

8 Rembrandt
This immaculate, good-value hotel has a wonderful antique breakfast room and spacious contemporary bedrooms that can accommodate up to six people. ✪ *Plantage Middenlaan 17, 1018 Dis. access • Map F4 • 020 627 2714 • www. hotelrembrandt.nl • €*

9 NH Schiller
Teenagers might put up with parents in this famous Art Deco hotel overlooking the neon glare of Rembrandtplein, once the meeting-place of artists and poets. There are family rooms, and the kids can escape to the buzzing Schiller Café. ✪ *Rembrandtplein 26, 1017 CV • Map N6 • 020 554 0700 • www.nh-hotels.co • Dis. access • €€€€*

10 Albus Grand
Parents may prefer old-world character, but children usually like their hotels to look spanking new, like this recently opened three-star hotel the Canal Ring. Some rooms sleep three or four and there is a brasserie for breakfast and snacks. ✪ *Vijzelstraat 49, 1017 HE • Map N6 • 020 530 6200 • www.albusgrandhotel.r • Dis. access • €€€*

Note: Unless otherwise stated, all hotels accept credit cards and have en-suite bathrooms.

Streetsmart

Price Categories

For a standard,
double room per
night (with breakfast
if included), taxes
and extra charges.

€ under €90
€€ €90–140
€€€ €140–200
€€€€ €200–250
€€€€€ over €250

wissôtel Amsterdam

10 Business Hotels

1 Swissôtel Amsterdam

he noise and bustle of
amrak is alleviated by
touch more style and
timacy than in most
ther business hotels in
e area. Bedrooms are
tylishly modern and
ell-insulated, and there
a fitness centre. ◊
amrak 96, 1012 LP • Map
3 • 020 522 3000 • www.
wissotel.com • Dis. access
€€€€

2 Radisson SAS

Situated around a
ramatic atrium, this
ell-run hotel takes up
ost of the street and
omprises several old
ouses, a paper factory
nd an 18th-century
carage, part of which
as become a lovely
andlelit bar. The hotel's
ealth and conference
entres are across the
bad, connected by a
nnel. ◊ Rusland 17, 1012
K • Map N4 • 020 623
231 • www.radissonsas.
om • Dis. access • €€€€€

3 Victoria Hotel Amsterdam

n the corner of Damrak
nd opposite Centraal
tation, this monumental
uilding has a surprising-
calm and gracious
terior. The hotel has a
usiness Centre, extens-
e conference facilities
nd a health and fitness
entre. ◊ Damrak 1-5, 1012
G • Map P1 • 020 623
255 • www.parkplaza
urope.com • Dis. access
€€€€€

4 Renaissance Amsterdam

A wide range of
facilities at surprisingly
reasonable rates
distinguish this central
hotel. The business
and conference centre
occupies a former
Lutheran church. The
hotel has a health
centre, brown café,
boat dock, car parking
and apartments, in
addition to the usual
bedrooms and suites.
◊ Kattengat 1, 1012 SZ •
Map N1 • 020 621 2223 •
www.renaissance
hotels.com/amsrd • Dis.
access • €€€€€

5 Crowne Plaza Amsterdam City Centre

A straightforward city-
centre business hotel
with good business
facilities and a leisure
centre, and the bonus of
Dorrius, a late 19th-
century Dutch restaurant
(see p58). ◊ Nieuwezijds
Voorburgwal 5, 1012 RC
• Map N1 • 020 620 0500
• www.amsterdam-city
centre.crowneplaza.com
• Dis. access • €€€€€

6 Okura

Handy for the RAI
Congresgebouw, the
Okura offers top-of-the-
range luxury and facilities
to business travellers. It
has four restaurants,
including the Ciel Bleu
perched on its 22nd floor.
◊ Ferdinand Bolstraat 333 •
020 678 7111 • www.okura.
nl • Dis. access • €€€€€

7 Dikker & Thijs Fenice

With interior decoration
in pinks, greys and blacks
to reflect its Art Deco
exterior, this long-
established hotel near
Leidseplein has more
individuality than most. ◊
Prinsengracht 444, 1017 KE
• Map L6 • 020 620 1212 •
www.dtfh.nl • €€€€

8 AMS Omega

With a vibrant colour
scheme in red and
orange, the Omega has
plenty of panache, plus
the bonus of a garden, a
roof terrace, and partic-
ularly accommodating
staff. ◊ Jacob Obrecht-
straat 33, 1071 KG • Map
C6 • 020 664 5182 •
www.ams.nl • €€€

9 Residence Le Coin

In the University District,
this smart new complex
of studio bedrooms, each
with kitchenette, is
patronized mainly by
visiting academics. ◊
Nieuwe Doelenstraat 5,
1012 CP • Map N5 • 020
524 6800 • €€

10 AMS Atlas

Friendly and efficient,
with business-like
bedrooms – though no
particular business
facilities – the Atlas, in
an interesting Art
Nouveau house near
Vondelpark, makes a
good budget choice. ◊
Van Eeghenstraat 64, 1071
GK • Map C6 • 020 676
6336 • www.ams.nl • €€€

Left **Engeland** Right **Quentin**

🔟 Gay Hotels

1 Engeland

A row of seven unusual houses in this hotel-packed street represent the architectural styles of seven different nations. The Engeland, a cosy, gay-friendly establishment, occupies the English "cottage" amongst them, plus the Netherlands house next door. ⊗ *Roemer Visscherstraat 30, 1054 EZ • Map C5 • 020 689 2323 • Dis. access • €€*

2 Quentin

A prime example of an Amsterdam hotel that, although not exclusively gay, extends a warm welcome to its many gay guests. Women in particular make this friendly, well-kept little hotel near Leidseplein their base, as do visiting musicians – Paradiso and Melkweg are nearby *(see p54–5)*. ⊗ *Leidsekade 89, 1017 PN • Map J6 • 020 626 2187 • www.quentin hotel.com • €€*

3 ITC

A long-established, exclusively gay hotel, the International Travel Club has a quiet, discreet atmosphere, with an attractive breakfast room overlooking Prinsengracht. The house is old and characterful, and no two rooms are the same. Accordingly, all of them are individually priced. ⊗ *Prinsengracht 1051, 1017 JE • Map E5 • 020 623 0230 • www.itc-hotel.com • €*

4 Greenwich Village

In the same gay enclave of Kerkstraat, the Greenwich Village provides simple, friendly accommodation at a very reasonable price. There are 11 clean but plain bedrooms. ⊗ *Kerkstraat 25, 1017 GA • Map L6 • 020 626 9746 • €*

5 Golden Bear

First opened in 1948, the Golden Bear has been a popular exclusively gay hotel ever since. With a pretty façade and 11 clean, neat rooms, some with shared facilities, it's situated in Kerkstraat – a street in the Canal Ring where there are several other gay venues. ⊗ *Kerkstraat 37, 1017 GB • Map L6 • 020 624 4785 • www.goldenbear.nl • €*

6 Waterfront

Bedrooms are a cut above at this smart, gay-friendly hotel within easy reach of the artistic treasures of the Museum Quarter and the historic centre. The distinctive reception room has a black-and-white floor and antique furniture. ⊗ *Singel 458, 1017 AW • Map M5 • 020 421 6621 • www. hotelwaterfront.nl • €€*

7 Sander

A gay-friendly hotel situated behind the Concertgebouw in the Museum Quarter. Though plain, most of the 20 rooms are spacious, some with features such as fireplaces and window seats. The breakfast room opens on to a pretty garden. ⊗ *Jacob Obrechtstraat 69 • Map C6 • 020 662 7574 • www. xs4all.nl/~htlsandr • Dis. access • €€*

8 Orfeo

A consistent favourite among Amsterdam's gay hotels, the Orfeo is centrally located near bustling Leidseplein. It has friendly, helpful owners, a convivial bar and free Finnish sauna. ⊗ *Leidse-kruisstraat 14, 1017 RH • Map D5 • 020 623 1347 • www.hotelorfeo.com • €*

9 Black Tulip

Only in Amsterdam an exclusive hotel, opened in 1998, for gay men into leather and bondage with appropriate equipment in each room. It's appropriately located too near the "leather area" and Centraal Station. ⊗ *Geldersekade 16, 1012 BH • Map Q2 • 020 427 0933 • www.blacktulip.nl • €€*

🔟 Flatmates Amsterdam

Not a hotel but a service offering a variety of accomodation: an apartment on Nieuwe Achtergracht (near the Theater Carré), a studio apartment in the Jordaan and an exclusively gay B&B on Java Eiland. ⊗ *020 620 1545 • www. flatmates.nl • €€*

 ***Note:** Unless otherwise stated, all hotels accept credit cards and have en-suite bathrooms.*

Price Categories

For a standard, double room per night (with breakfast if included), taxes and extra charges.

€	under €90
€€	€90–140
€€€	€140–200
€€€€	€200–250
€€€€€	over €250

Amstel Botel

🔟 Budget Hotels

1 Fantasia
Close to the Amstel, in a peaceful canal, the Fantasia Hotel is clean and well organized. The rooms on the top floor have the most character, but all rooms have a shower and a phone. ✆ Nieuwe Keizersgracht 16, 1018 DR • Map Q6 • 020 623 8259 • www.fantasia-hotel.com • €

2 De Munck
Originally built for a ship's captain and within sailing distance of the Amstel, an otherwise traditional interior has been given a dose of 1960s retro. Rooms in the De Munck are airy and clean, and there is both a bar and a garden. ✆ Achtergracht 3, 1017 WL • Map E5 • 020 623 6283 • www.hoteldemunck.com • €€

3 Amstel Botel
The idea of staying on a boat has a certain charm, but the downside of the Amstel Botel is that the rooms (or cabins if you prefer) on this floating hotel are small, and even the view over the water is dull. The upside is getting three-star accommodation at a very reasonable price – and being near the station means there are trams and buses on your doorstep. ✆ Oosterdoks-kade 2–4, 1011 AE • Map Q2 • 020 626 4247 • www.amstelbotel.com • Dis. access • €

4 Van Ostade Bicycle Hotel
Clean, cheap, simple rooms away from the tourist traps, bikes for rent, free maps, and friendly advice on routes and sights attract a young clientele to this popular hotel. What might be a lounge elsewhere is "a chill-out zone" here in De Pijp. ✆ Van Ostadestraat 123, 1072 SV • 020 679 3452 • www.bicyclehotel.com • no credit cards • €

5 Museumzicht
You can peer down into the lovely Rijksmuseum garden from the plain rooms at the back of this modest hotel occupying the top floors of a Victorian house. The Museumzicht's greatest asset is its splendid location. ✆ Jan Luykenstraat 22, 1071 CN • Map C5 • 020 671 2954 • €

6 Acacia
Steep stairs, simple rooms (some with epic canal views) and a pleasant breakfast room are a quarter of an hour's walk away from the city centre, in Jordaan. The charming owners also offer self-catering studios, and a houseboat on a nearby canal. ✆ Lindengracht 251, 1015 KH • Map C2 • 020 622 1460 • www.hotelacacia.nl • €

7 ISC Keizersgracht
Great location, rooms for up to four people and budget prices sound like a pipe dream, but this welcoming hotel at the station end of the Keizersgracht has them all – and a bar and restaurant to boot. ✆ Keizersgracht 15–17, 1015 CC • Map M1 • 020 625 1364 • €

8 De Admiraal
At the junction of Herengracht and Reguliersgracht, and with views over both, this friendly hotel's beamed bedrooms are bigger than most, and it's close enough to the nightlife for breakfast to be optional. ✆ Herengracht 563, 1017 CD • Map N6 • 020 626 2150 • €

9 Asterisk
Far from the madding crowd on a residential backstreet, this spruce little hotel has decent-sized bedrooms and a touch of style in its 19th-century moulded ceilings. Breakfast is included in the room price if you pay cash. ✆ Den Texstraat 16, 1017 ZA • Map E6 • 020 624 1768 • www.asteriskhotel.nl • €

10 Hegra
Its prime location on the lovely Herengracht, its prices and the warmth of its welcome make up for the (comfortable) rooms being rather on the small side. ✆ Herengracht 269, 1016 BJ • Map L3 • 020 623 7877 • hegra@wxs.nl • €

General Index

Acknowledgements

Main Contributors

Fiona Duncan and Leonie Glass are a British travel-writing team of 15 years standing. They are co-authors of three guides in Duncan Petersen's *3-D City Guides* series, including a guide to Amsterdam; *Paris Walks*, in the *On Foot City Guides* series; and several *Charming Small Hotel* guides.

Additional Contributors

Pip Farquharson (Top 10 Bars, Performing Arts Venues and Clubs; all Around Town listings) is a journalist and long-time inhabitant of Amsterdam. She publishes her own alternative listings guide to the city, *Shark*.

Rodney Bolt (Top 10 Cafés, Bars and Restaurants) also lives in Amsterdam. He is a novelist, and author of several Cadogan travel guides.

Produced by DP Services, a division of DUNCAN PETERSEN PUBLISHING LTD

Project Editor Chris Barstow
Designer Janis Utton
Picture Researcher Lily Sellar
Indexer Hilary Bird

Main Photographer Anthony Souter
Additional Photography Max Alexander, Steve Gorton, Rupert Horrox, Kim Sayer, Clive Streeter

Illustrator chrisorr.com

Maps Dominic Beddow, Simonetta Giori (Draughtsman Ltd)

FOR DORLING KINDERSLEY
Publisher Douglas Amrine
Senior Art Editor Marisa Renzullo
Senior Cartographic Editor Casper Morris
DTP Jason Little
Production Sarah Dodd
Picture Librarian Charlotte Oster

Picture Credits

t-top; tc-top centre; tl-top left; tr-top right; cla-centre left above; ca-centre above; cra-centre right above; cl-centre left; c-centre; cr-centre right; clb-centre left below; cb-centre below; crb-centre right below; bl-bottom left; bc-bottom centre; bcl-bottom centre left; bcr-bottom centre right; br-bottom right; d-detail.

Every effort has been made to trace the copyright holders and we apologize in advance for any unintentional omissions. We would be pleased to insert the appropriate acknowledgements in any subsequent edition of this publication.

Works of art have been reproduced with the permission of the following copyright holders: ©ADAGP, Paris and DACS, London 2002 *Portrait of Bernard's Grandmother*, 1887, by Emile Bernard 18b; ©DACS, 2002, *Children with Dog*, 1950, by Karel Appel 47bl; ©Munch Museum/Munch-Ellingsen Group, BONO, Oslo, DACS, London 2002, *Two Women on the Beach*, 1898, by Edvard Munch 14tl.

The publishers would like to thank the following individuals, companies and picture libraries for permission to reproduce their photographs:

AKG LONDON: 38tr, 49rd, *Dutch Battle Ships*, 1863, by Ludolf Backhuysen 27b; Residenzmuseum, Munich, *Peter the Great*, 1717 by Jean Marc Nattier 10c; Kunsthistorisches Museum, Erich Lessing, *Allegory of Painting*, c1665-66, by Jan Vermeer 46tl.

AMSTERDAM ARENA: 71rd, 129tr.

AMSTERDAMS HISTORISCH MUSEUM: 7cla, 24t, 25tc, 25cra, 25bl, 26b, 40b, 107b; *Bird's Eye View of Amsterdam*, 1538, by Cornelis Anthonisz 24c; *The Return to Amsterdam of the Second Expedition to the East Indies*, 1599, by Hendrik Cornelisz Vroom 24b; *The Anatomy Lesson of Dr Jan Deijman*, 1656, by Rembrandt van Rijn 25c; *Dam Square with the New Town Hall under Construction* 1656, by Johannes Lingelbach 26tl; *Portrait of 17 Guards* by Cornelis Anthonisz 26tr; *Silver Marriage Cup* by Gerrit Valek 27c; *Arrival of Napoleon at Dam Square*, 1811 by Matheus I van Bree 38tl; *Tulp en Spin* by B. Assteijn 83b.

AFF/AFS AMSTERDAM, THE
ETHERLANDS: 7bl, 32tl, 32br, 32-33c,
3cr, 33b, 47br.

MSTERDAM, VAN GOGH MUSEUM:
ïew of Prins Hendrikkade by Claude
Monet 18tc; Vincent van Gogh Foundation
9cl; Vase with Sunflowers, 1889, by
incent van Gogh 6cb, 16c; The Potato
aters, 1889 by Vincent van Gogh 16cb;
, Pair of Shoes, 1885, by Vincent van Gogh
7tr; Self Portrait as an Artist, 1887, by
incent van Gogh 17ca; Wheatfield with
rows, 1890, by Vincent van Gogh 17b,
6tr; Portrait of van Gogh by Paul Gauguin
Btl; Self Portrait with a Portrait of Bernard,
.es Misérables', 1888, by Paul Gauguin
Btr; ©ADAGP, Paris and DACS, London
002 Portrait of Bernard's Grandmother,
887, by Emile Bernard 18b; The Bedroom
t Arles, 1888, by Vincent van Gogh 19b.

IJBELS MUSEUM: Ernest Annyas 99t,
01br.

OBRA MUSEUM VOOR MODERNE
UNST, AMSTELVEEN: ©DACS, 2002,
'hildren with Dog, 1950, by Karel Appel 47bl.

'OSTER DIAMONDS: 116b, 117tr.

ETTY IMAGES: 47tr.

AN DERWIG ARCHITECTUUR
IOTOGRAFIE: 126b.

OODS HISTORISCH MUSEUM: Jeroen
ooter 48tl, 48tr, 48b.

ONINKLIJK INSTITUT VOOR DE TROPEN:
27t.

ONINKLIJK THEATER CARRÉ: Rob Liot
22tl.

MARY EVANS PICTURE LIBRARY: 39br.

MUSEUM AMSTELKRING: Gert Jan van
Kooij 6b, 20tl, 20cb, 20br, 20-21c, 21cr,
1cb, 21bl, 82c.

MUSEUM HET REMBRANDTHUIS: 41t, 76tr.

MUSEUM VAN LOON: Maarten Brinkgreve

7cr, 30tl, 30cb, 30cr, 30-31c, 31cr, 31bc;
The Romantic Double Portrait, 1791, by
J.F.A Tischbein 31bl.

NEDERLANDS SCHEEPVAARTMUSEUM,
AMSTERDAM: 40tr, Plan of Amsterdam,
1648, 11b.

PA PHOTOS: 39bl.

PATHÉ TUSCHINSKI, AMSTERDAM: 49t,
106cr.

PICTURE BOX: 64tl, 64b, 70tl, 70tr, 70b;
Cuypers, Fotografie Igno 42tl; Amerens
Hedwich 23tc, 23c, 40tl; Leeden van der
Henk 71tl.

RIJKSMUSEUM, AMSTERDAM: 13cr,
13cb, 14tr; The Kitchen Maid, 1658, by
Johannes Vermeer 6cl, 12b; The Windmill
at Wijk, 1670, by Jacob van Ruisdael 13tr;
Winter Landscape with Skaters, 1608, by
Hendrick Avercamp 13cra; Portrait of
Woman in Turkish Costume, 1745, by Jean-
Etienne Liotard 13bl; ©Munch Museum/
Munch-Ellingsen Group, BONO, Oslo,
DACS, London 2002, Two Women on the
Beach, 1898, by Edvard Munch 14tl; Gallant
Conversation, 1654, by Gerard ter Borch II
14tc; Self Portrait as St Paul, 1661, by
Rembrandt van Rijn 15c; Company of Frans
Banning Cocq and Willem van Ruytenburch
known as The Night Watch, 1642, by
Rembrandt van Rijn 15b; Self Portrait at a
Young Age, 1628, by Rembrandt van Rijn 46c.

THEATER MUSEUM, AMSTERDAM: 67bl.

WORLD OF AJAX: 127b.

JACKET: Front – DK PICTURE LIBRARY b,
cla; Max Alexander clb; Steve Gorton tc;
Kim Sayer main image. Back - CORBIS,
Dave Bartruff tl; DK PICTURE LIBRARY tr;
Max Alexander tc.

All other images © Dorling Kindersley. See
www.DKimages.com for more information.

Phrase Book

In an Emergency

Help!	**Help!**	Help
Stop!	**Stop!**	Stop
Call a doctor.	**Haal een dokter.**	Haal uhn dok-tur
Call an ambulance.	**Bel een ambulance.**	Bell uhn ahm-bew-luhns-uh
Call the police.	**Roep de politie.**	Roop duh poe-leet-see
Call the fire brigade.	**Roep de brandweer.**	Roop duh brahnt-vheer

Communication Essentials

Yes	**Ja**	Yaa
No	**Nee**	Nay
Please	**Alstublieft**	Ahls-tew-bleeft
Thank you	**Dank u**	Dahnk-ew
Excuse me	**Pardon**	Pahr-don
Hello	**Hallo**	Hallo
Goodbye	**Dag**	Dahgh
Good night	**Slaap lekker**	slapp lek-kah
morning	**Morgen**	Mor-ghuh
afternoon	**Middag**	Mid-dahgh
evening	**Avond**	Ah-vohnd
What?	**Wat?**	Vhat
When?	**Wanneer?**	Vhan-eer
Why?	**Waarom?**	Vhaar-om
Where?	**Waar?**	Vhaar

Useful Phrases

How are you?	**Hoe gaat het ermee?**	Hoo ghaat het er-may
Very well, thank you.	**Heel goed, dank u.**	Hayl ghoot, dahnk ew
How do you do?	**Hoe maakt u het?**	Hoo maakt ew het
That's fine.	**Prima.**	Pree-mah
Where is/are ...?	**Waar is/zijn?**	Vhaar iss/zayn
How do I get to ...?	**Hoe kom ik naar ...?**	Hoo kom ik naar
Do you speak English?	**Spreekt u engels?**	Spraykt ew eng-uhls
I don't understand.	**Ik snap het niet.**	Ik snahp het neet
I'm sorry.	**Sorry.**	Sorry

Shopping

How much does this cost?	**Hoeveel kost dit?**	Hoo-vayl kost dit?
I would like ...	**Ik wil graag ...**	Ik vhil ghraakh
Do you have ...?	**Heeft u ...?**	Hayft ew
Do you take credit cards?	**Neemt u credit cards aan?**	Naymt ew credit cards aan
Do you take traveller's cheques?	**Neemt u reischeques aan?**	Naymt ew raiys-sheks
What time do you open/close?	**Hoe laat gaat u open/dicht?**	Hoo laat ghaat ew opuh/dikht
this one	**deze**	day-zuh
that one	**Die**	dee
expensive	**duur**	dewr
cheap	**goedkoop**	ghoot-koap
size	**maat**	maat
white	**wit**	vhit
black	**zwart**	zvhahrt
red	**rood**	roat
yellow	**geel**	ghayl
green	**groen**	ghroon
blue	**blauw**	blah-ew

Types of Shop

antique shop	**antiekwinkel**	ahn-teek-vhin-k
bakery	**bakker**	bah-ker
bank	**bank**	bahnk
bookshop	**boekwinkel**	book-vhin-kul
butcher	**slager**	slaakh-er
cake shop	**banketbakkerij**	bahnk-et-bahk-er-aiy
cheese shop	**kaaswinkel**	kaas-vhin-kul
chemist	**apotheek**	ah-poe-taiyk
chip shop	**patatzaak**	pah-taht-zaak
delicatessen	**delicatessen**	daylee-kah-tes-suh
department store	**warenhuis**	vhaar-uh-houw
fishmonger	**viswinkel**	viss-vhin-kul
greengrocer	**groenteboer**	ghroon-tuh-boe
hairdresser	**kapper**	kah-per
market	**markt**	mahrkt
newsagent	**krantenwinkel**	krahn-tuh-vhin-kul
post office	**postkantoor**	pohst-kahn-tor
shoe shop	**schoenenwinkel**	sghoo-nuh-vhin-kul
supermarket	**schoenenwinkel**	sghoo-nuh-vhin-kul
tobacconist	**sigarenwinkel**	see-ghaa-ruh-vhin-kul
travel agent	**reisburo**	raiys-bew-roa

Sightseeing

art gallery	**gallerie**	ghaller-ee
bus station	**busstation**	buhs-stah-shown
bus ticket	**strippenkaart**	strip-puh-kaahi
cathedral	**kathedraal**	kah-tuh-draal
church	**kerk**	kehrk
closed on public holidays	**op feestdagen gesloten**	op fayst-daa-ghuh ghuh-slow-tuhi
day return	**dagretour**	dahgh-ruh-tour
garden	**tuin**	touwn
library	**bibliotheek**	bee-bee-yo-tay
museum	**museum**	mew-zay-uhm
railway station	**station**	stah-shown
return ticket	**retourtje**	ruh-tour-tyuh
single journey	**enkeltje**	eng-kuhl-tyuh
tourist information	**VVV**	fay fay fay
town hall	**stadhuis**	staht-houws
train	**trein**	traiyn

Staying in a Hotel

Do you have a vacant room?	**Zijn er nog kamers vrij?**	Zaiyn er nokh kaamers vray
double room	**een twees persoonskamer**	uhn tvhay-per soans-kaa-mei
with double bed	**met een twee persoonsbed**	met uhn tvhay-per-soans behi
twin room	**een kamer met een lits-jumeaux**	uhn kaa-mer met uhn lee-zjoo-moh
single room	**eenpersoons-kamer**	ayn-per-soans-kaa-mer
room with bath	**kamer met bad**	kaa-met baht
shower	**douche**	doosh
porter	**kruier**	krouw-yuh
I have a reservation.	**Ik heb gereseveerd.**	Ik hehp ghuh-ray-sehr-veert

Eating Out

Have you got a table?	**Is er een tafel vrij?**	Iss ehr uhn tah-fuhl vraiy
I'd like to reserve a table.	**Ik wil een tafel reserveren.**	Ik vhil uhn tah-fuhl ray-sehr-veer-uh
breakfast	**het ontbijt**	het ont-baiyt
lunch	**de lunch**	duh lernsh
dinner	**het diner**	het dee-nay
The bill, please.	**Mag ik afrekenen.**	Mukh ik ahf-ray-kuh-nuh
waitress	**serveerster**	sehr-veer-ster
waiter	**ober**	oh-ber
menu	**de kaart**	duh kaahrt
starter, first course	**het voorgerecht**	het vohr-ghuh-rekht
main course	**het hoofdgerecht**	het hoaft-ghuh-rekht
dessert	**het nagerecht**	het naa-ghuh-rekht
cover charge	**het couvert**	het koo-vehr
wine list	**de wijnkaart**	duh vhaiyn-kaart
glass	**het glas**	het ghlahss
bottle	**de fles**	duh fless
knife	**het mes**	het mess
fork	**de vork**	duh fork
spoon	**de lepel**	duh lay-pul

Menu Decoder

aardappels	aard-uppuhls	potatoes
azijn	aah-zaiyn	vinegar
biefstuk	beef-stuhk	steak
bier, pils	beer, pilss	beer
boter	boater	butter
brood	broat	bread
cake, taart, gebak	'cake', taahrt, ghuh-bahk	cake, pastry
chocola	show-coa-laa	chocolate
citroen	see-troon	lemon
cocktail	cocktail	cocktail
droog	droakh	dry
eend	aynt	duck
ei	aiy	egg
garnalen	ghahr-naah-luh	prawns
gebakken	ghuh-bah-ken	fried
gegrild	ghuh-ghrillt	grilled
gekookt	ghuh-koakt	boiled
gepocheerd	ghuh-posh-eert	poached
groenten	ghroon-tuh	vegetables
ham	hahm	ham
haring	haa-ring	herring
hutspot	huht-spot	hot pot
ijs	aiyss	ice, ice cream
jenever	yuh-nay-vhur	gin
kaas	kaas	cheese
kabeljauw	kah-buhl-youw	cod
kip	kip	chicken
koffie	coffee	coffee
kool, rode of witte	coal, roe-duh off vhit-uh	cabbage, red or white
kroket	crow-ket	ragout in breadcrumbs
lamsvlees	lahms-flayss	lamb
mineraalwater	meener-aahl-vhaater	mineral water
mosterd	moss-tehrt	mustard
olie	oh-lee	oil
pannekoek	pah-nuh-kook	pancake
patat frites	pah-taht freet	chips
peper	pay-per	pepper
poffertjes	poffer-tyuhs	tiny buckwheat pancakes
rijst	raiyst	rice

rijsttafel	raiys-tah-ful	Indonesian meal
rode wijn	roe-duh vhaiyn	red wine
rookworst	roak-vhorst	smoked sausage
rundvlees	ruhnt-flayss	beef
saus	souwss	sauce
schaaldieren	skaahl-deeh-ruh	shellfish
scherp	skehrp	hot (spicy)
schol	sghol	plaice
soep	soup	soup
stamppot	stahm-pot	sausage stew
suiker	souw-ker	sugar
thee	tay	tea
tosti	toss-tee	cheese on toast
uien	ouw-yuh	onions
uitsmijter	ouht-smaiy-ter	fried egg on bread with ham
varkensvlees	vahr-kuhns-flayss	pork
vers fruit	fehrss frouwt	fresh fruit
verse jus	vehr-suh zjhew	fresh orange juice
vis	fiss	fish/seafood
vlees	flayss	meat
water	vhaa-ter	water
witte wijn	vhih-tuh vhaiyn	white wine
worst	vhorst	sausage
zout	zouwt	salt

Numbers

1	**een**	ayn
2	**twee**	tvhay
3	**drie**	dree
4	**vier**	feer
5	**vijf**	faiyf
6	**zes**	zess
7	**zeven**	zay-vuh
8	**acht**	ahkht
9	**negen**	nay-guh
10	**tien**	teen
11	**elf**	elf
12	**twaalf**	tvhaalf
13	**dertien**	dehr-teen
14	**veertien**	feer-teen
15	**vijftien**	faiyf-teen
16	**zestien**	zess-teen
17	**zeventien**	zayvuh-teen
18	**achtien**	ahkh-teen
19	**negentien**	nay-ghuh-teen
20	**twintig**	tvhin-tuhh
21	**eenentwintig**	aynuh-tvhin-tukh
30	**dertig**	dehr-tukh
40	**veertig**	feer-tukh
50	**vijftig**	faiyt-tukh
60	**zestig**	zess-tukh
70	**zeventig**	zay-vuh-tukh
80	**tachtig**	tahkh-tukh
90	**negentig**	nayguh-tukh
100	**honderd**	hohn-durt
1000	**duizend**	douw-zuhnt
1,000,000	**miljoen**	mill-yoon

Time

one minute	**een minuut**	uhn meen-ewt
one hour	**een uur**	uhn ewr
a day	**een dag**	uhn dahgh
Monday	**maandag**	maan-dahgh
Tuesday	**dinsdag**	dins-dahgh
Wednesday	**woensdag**	vhoons-dahgh
Thursday	**donderdag**	donder-dahgh
Friday	**vrijdag**	vraiy-dahgh
Saturday	**zaterdag**	zaater-dahgh
Sunday	**zondag**	zon-dahgh

Selected Street Index